Intuitive You!

Psychic and Personal Development

From Psychic and Spiritual Advisor

Rev. Kristina L. Bloom

Moonbow Publications, Menomonee Falls, Wisconsin

Copyright ©2019 Kristina Bloom

All rights reserved. No part of this publication may be reproduced, stored in a retrieval system, or transmitted, in any form or by any means, electronic, mechanical, photocopying, recording, or otherwise, without prior written permission of the publisher and author, Kristina Bloom.

Published in in the United States of America by Moonbow Publications

Printed in the United States of America by Ingram Spark

Cover design by Kristina Bloom

Catalog-in-Publication Data for this book is available from the Library of Congress.

ISBN 978-1-7342798-0-1

While the author has made every effort to provide correct internet addresses at the time of publication, neither the publisher nor the author assumes any responsibility for errors, or for changes that occur after publication. Further, the published does not have any control over and does not assume any responsibility for the author or third-party websites or their contents.

http://kristinabloom.com

Table of Contents

Dedication iii
Acknowledgment v
Forward vii
Author's Note xi
Introduction 1
Chapter 1: An Introduction to Developing Your Psychic Abilities 4
Chapter 2: Discerning Energy and Intuition 40
Chapter 3: Mediumship 62
Chapter 4: Managing and Manipulating Energy 76
Chapter 5: Paranormal Investigation 98
Chapter 6: The Paranormal Investigation Field Trip 117
A Note from the Author 122
Author Contact Information 123
Index

Dedication

The entire *Intuitive You!* Psychic Development program is dedicated to a courageous woman named Suzanne who wanted to learn mediumship in order to communicate with her son who had passed unexpectedly. Without her having the courage to ask for that teaching this program would not exist.

Thank you Suzanne for stepping up and reaching out.

Eternal Gratitude,

Rev. Kristina Bloom

Psychic and Spiritual Advisor

Acknowledgment

Dean Graziosi said in his book, *Millionaire Success Habits*, that it's important to have a team of people who support you in your mission and realizing your dreams. And what a team I have! I am blessed to be surrounded by so many people who believe in me and what I'm capable of accomplishing!

Starting with my husband, Jonathon Anderson, who in his own unique way pushes me to be a better person, partner and business owner. My kids, Logan Jacobson and Chris Johnson who have been watching me alternately fail and succeed as I've been growing the concept for this book for the last twelve years.

All of my hundreds of Intuitive You! students over the years who have honored me by taking my classes and honored themselves by continuing on their own spiritual journeys. The students who have continued through the Intuitive You! program all the way to the end and become Certified teachers of the program. You can find them listed on my website, http://kristinabloom.com.

Marla McKenna and Sue Carlson, the two brilliant women who edited this book. Sue Carlson for the layout and design of the book. Julie Kucharkski, artist extraordinaire, for the cover art. Sherry Levitsch for the cover design and the great website she created for me. And finally, my Spirit Guides, who gave me this entire program through channeled writing, week by week, lesson by lesson. Without them I would have nothing to write about!

This is my Dream Team without whom this published book would not have happened. Thank you all!

Rev. Kristina L. Bloom

Forward

I am so excited that you are reading this book!

It was about a dozen years ago when I first realized that I was truly psychic. I wasn't one of those who grew up seeing dead people, a prodigy who read for her grandmother's friends, or who predicted big events. Or at least not consciously. I mean, I did always seem to know who was on the phone before things like caller ID existed or even answering machines. It wasn't until I turned 50 that my abilities came flooding in in a way that I could no longer ignore and no longer wanted to. So, I searched online for a class of some sort. Overwhelmed at the number of offerings that popped up, I asked Spirit to help me decide. I heard "keep scrolling, keep scrolling, keep scrolling, stop." Spirit led me to one of Kristina's very first Intuitive You! classes. Having learned not to ignore Spirit, I signed up for her six-week course. You know, just for kicks, just to see what all the fuss is about. Just to see how I can call on this *thing* more proactively. Little did I know then that I would stay with Kristina for two full years.

When I met Kristina Bloom, I was relieved to see that she was that rare combination of gifted psychic who also remembers to pay the power bill. She treated her class like a contract with students and treated each of us like the incredible souls that we are.

Under Kristina's tutelage, I learned how my intuition shows up for me and was introduced to so many other modalities that learning to develop these skills has led me to other teachers and a whole community of like-minded, supportive people.

Living in one of the major tech hubs in the world, finding a like-minded community was no small gift.

Then she threw me into the arena – a psychic fair -- nudge that she is. "I can't charge people money for this. That seems like such a big promise to make to someone – that I'm that good." Kristina's answer? "You're reading the room anyway. You might as well get paid for it." She was right. I was ready and I was good at it. So, I raised my prices. It is also one of the many ways I have learned to be in service to others. This information is powerful and its healing powers are not to be underestimated.

With Kristina's permission, I have personally taught Intuitive You! I marvel every time at how much information is contained within. Each workshop deepens my own understanding as well as my appreciation for Kristina. You are in good hands following her instruction.

If you are cracking open this book, you are ready. You might think you're just curious. You might think "I can't do this." Or even "I'm good if I don't take this too seriously." All are perfectly acceptable reasons to put your toe in the water of investigating your intuitive self. My suggestion is to let go of all preconceived ideas of what it means to be intuitive or psychic. Just be open. Don't compare yourself to your friend, classmate, or skills that others in your family may possess. You might miss out on the very best part of your intuition. Everyone is slightly different. Everyone is better at some modalities and less so with others. Curiosity is your best friend on this adventure. Let go and allow.

When doctors graduate from medical school, they go into medical practice, not perfection. Practice, practice, practice. This is a skill that takes time to build, understand, and control. If you only do this for kicks, you may only get a kick out of it. For me, it changed the course of my life.

Mary Gleason

Professional Psychic Medium, Licensed Hypnotherapist, and Intuition Coach

Author's Note

Welcome to *Intuitive You!*

Whether you are just beginning to explore your own spirituality or you are looking for ways to expand your spiritual experiences you have been lead here, and we are honored to be part of your journey!

This class began in 2007 in Bellevue, Washington at the request of a dear woman who wanted to communicate with her deceased son. I have since taught it in six states and have expanded *Intuitive You!* from a one level - six week class to a three level - 24 week course. Each student may take as many of the levels as supports the student's own spiritual path. I also offer a teacher certification course for those who want to share this enlightening course with others. Whatever number of levels fits your needs, our instructors will always honor you as you follow your own intuition. We are here to help you and guide you as much or as little as you need during your time with us.

I developed *Intuitive You!* with the belief that *everyone* is intuitive. Intuition works in countless ways and our goal is to help you determine how yours works so that you can decide how you want to use it and in what capacity. During the first level, *Intuitive You! 101*, you will become familiar with a few different "tools" that can help you develop your intuitive abilities. Some may resonate with you while others may not. That's why we introduce them so you can try them and decide for yourself. You will also learn about your own personal energy and how to effectively manage it for your highest good.

As you continue to *Intuitive You! The Next Level*, your personal energy management will expand to basic vibratory healing, aligning with manifestation, learning about Spirit Guides, meeting your personal Spirit Guides, and a past/other life exploration. With the introduction of each new skill, you will gain more awareness of your own Divine connection to the Universe as well as to other beings here on Earth.

The course is progressive at all levels so it is best to commit to each level fully when you decide to take the class. The classes will serve you best if you take them in order from the beginning regardless of your previous experience. It is a proven system of personal growth and development as much as it is for intuitive growth and development. You will discover how powerful your intentions and personal energy can be when you learn how to use them in Love and Light with confidence.

Blessings,

Rev. Kristina Bloom

Introduction

Hello and welcome to your *Intuitive You!* psychic development class. Be prepared to have fun, amaze yourself with your own intuitive and energetic abilities, and get to know your classmates!

Since the entire *Intuitive You!* curriculum is based on the belief that everyone has intuitive abilities, you will have ample opportunity to experiment with different ways to experience how your intuition works for you. We encourage you to have fun with what you learn and discover about yourself throughout the course. Let yourself be awed by what you can do!

I encourage you to keep a journal of your experiences as you progress through the class. We've provided a blank page at the end of each lesson for you to take notes. Feel free to use this as your journal if you like. The journal is for your own record and you don't have to share it with anyone unless you choose to do so. Use the journal to make note of dreams, any paranormal activity that you notice, how your relationships are changing… anything that you feel is important to your intuitive and personal process.

It is in your best interest to be kind and gentle with yourself as you develop your intuition. Judging yourself based on comparison to others is simply not helpful to you or anyone else. You will quickly realize that a large portion of psychic ability is how you perceive, understand and relay intuitive messages. Because of this, people who are naturally cautious will be so in sharing messages, those who are naturally more bold will be bold in relaying messages. It doesn't mean that anyone is a "better" psychic than the other, it just means that some people may be more confident in sharing what they perceive.

Are you using this book as the text for an in-person or online *Intuitive You!* class?

Personal insights are welcome in class, and you will likely become more comfortable sharing them as you get to know your classmates. Please avoid comparisons and self-deprecation as both can be detrimental to the rest of the class and to yourself. When you realize you could improve in some areas, we hope that you will choose to experience it as an "aha moment" rather than a reason to feel badly. Your instructor is here to support, as well as to educate and guide you without judgment, and to help you with whatever may be in the way of your highest and best experience.

I developed *Intuitive You!* as an interactive class. If you have a question, please feel free to ask it. If you have a comment or opinion about the class or the material offered in it, please feel free to share it. We all learn from each other. What you have to share is valuable! Discussions open new avenues of understanding for you, your fellow students and your teacher. Discussions also help the teacher to make sure that everyone understands the material that's being presented.

Whether you are using this book on your own or as part of a class, you will find it to be a practical guide to managing your own energy, enhancing your personal spiritual growth, and understanding more about how your intuition works for you.

Chapter 1: An Introduction to Developing Your Psychic Abilities

When you first learn about how intuition works it helps to understand the different ways that people experience it. Everyone's intuitive nature is unique. Communication with the metaphysical world can seem simple or complex depending on your level of understanding.

Let's start by defining "metaphysical". Some of the definitions found on dictionary.com define metaphysical as "incorporeal; supernatural" and "…having the form of an empirical hypothesis, but in fact immune from empirical testing…". Metaphysics covers many topics, from mediumship (communication with those who've left this physical life) to quantum physics and the theory of a multi-verse rather than just one universe. That's a lot of ground to cover, and we're not going to do it all at once!

Intuitive You! begins with learning to recognize when we are experiencing communication, whether from a loved one who is beyond our physical realm, spirit guides, angels or some other source.

You may experience metaphysical or paranormal communication in different ways: clairvoyance, clairaudience, clairsentience,

Chapter 1

Developing Your Psychic Abilities

clairalience, and clairgustance. As we explore the meanings and subtleties of these words, you are likely to realize which of them you already have and which you may want to try to develop. Most people experience more than one of these phenomena and sometimes more than one of them simultaneously. Read the descriptions below and make notes regarding how you experience any of these types of communication.

Your Notes

_____

_____

_____

_____

_____

_____

_____

_____

_____

_____

_____

Clairvoyance

Clairvoyance translates to "clear seeing". Those who can see ghosts, spirits, spirit guides, angels, or simply energy in different forms. Very few people see these entities as solid objects outside of their own physical bodies. Most people who are clairvoyant see images in their own minds. Sometimes the images seem to be "projected", as if the entity is standing near someone else or in a "location" away from the "seer". Think of this like a holographic image or an image from a slide or movie projector. Some see only colors in a variety of ways. Some see shapes, letters, or numbers. The metaphysical world will attempt to communicate in any way that makes sense to the receiver of the communication, which is why our experiences are so individual.

Things to think about:

- *How does clairvoyance look for you?*
- *If you are a "seer", describe what it's like for you.*
- *This section is for you to become clear about your own experiences, so make sure to include details that may help you as you develop your intuitive abilities.*

Your Notes
_____

_____

Chapter 1
Developing Your Psychic Abilities

Clairaudience

Clairaudience is "clear hearing". This can mean anything from hearing a door close in an empty room to having actual conversations with non-corporeal beings. Clairaudients give varied descriptions of their experiences, including strange or unidentifiable noises. Others hear clear messages, either for themselves or others, and can clearly identify the source of the messages. Sometimes the message is clear and the source is not. With all types of intuition, the variables are numerous. Clairaudience, however, can sometimes literally be like being blind…the voice can be there but without visual confirmation. Sometimes we get lucky have have both auditory and visual messages simultaneously.

Things to Think About:

- *How does clairaudience sound to you?*
- *Be specific to help you become clear about how your abilities work for you.*

Your Notes

_____

_____

_____

_____

Chapter 1
Developing Your Psychic Abilities

Clairecognizance

For some, the messages come in the form of a thought that seems to be in someone else's "voice" or is a thought that they wouldn't ordinarily think. A profound thought simply occurs to you.

It can come as an idea, an inspiration, a warning or any number of other ways, but it is generally helpful to you or someone else. Often, but not always, claircognizance comes after quiet contemplation or meditation though it may come hours later.

Things to think about:

- *List and describe all the ways Claircognizance comes to you.*

Your Notes

_____

_____

_____

_____

_____

_____

_____

Chapter 1
Developing Your Psychic Abilities

Clairsentience

Clairsentience means "clear feeling" and is probably the most common way people experience intuition. Even though the definition includes the word "clear", the messages sometimes don't feel all that clear!

Clairsentience includes gut feelings, empathy, a sense of being watched, goosebumps, feeling energy shifts, a knowing, temperature changes (usually chills), feeling like something has touched you, and can even include a sense that something should be common sense! All of these sensations give information, although that information can seem vague. Getting confirmation from someone else can help you to discern the meaning of such communication. If you are doing a psychic reading for someone you can ask them for confirmation, which can help you to gain clarity.

Things to think about:

- *List and describe all the different ways Clairsentience feels to you?*

Your Notes

_____

_____

_____

_____

Chapter 1
Developing Your Psychic Abilities

Clairalience

Clairalience means to smell clearly. Sometimes we get a whiff of something that smells familiar even though there is nothing in the immediate environment to account for it. The smell will usually remind you, or the person for whom you are doing an intuitive reading, of someone or some situation in particular. Clairalience happens most often during mediumship, communication with someone who crossed over, and is clear communication at least to the point of knowing who is contacting you. For example your grandmother's favorite perfume or the smell of a particular type of food will tell you clearly who exactly wants to speak with you.

Things to think about:
- *Have you ever experienced clairalience?*
- *What did you smell?*
- *Who did it remind you of?*

Your Notes

_____

_____

_____

_____

_____

_____

Chapter 1
Developing Your Psychic Abilities

Clairgustance

If you've ever had a sudden taste in your mouth, and hadn't recently eaten or drank anything, then you have experienced *clairegustance*. Often the taste that appears in your mouth will hold a memory for you, like your mom's cookies, indicating communication. The whole experience kind of feels like *deja vu* for your taste buds! This type of intuition is pretty rare, and is experienced by relatively few people.

Things to Think About:

- *Have you ever had a taste in your mouth that indicated spirit communication?*
- *What was it like?*
- *Did it bring any particular people or experiences to mind?*

Your Notes

_____
_____
_____
_____
_____
_____
_____

Chapter 1
Developing Your Psychic Abilities

How Do I Know the Communication is Real?

Now that we've covered a number of ways in which intuition presents itself, how do you know if the communication is real or imagined? This is called discernment; learning how to distinguish actual communication from our imaginations. One easy way to discern whether the communication is real or imagined is to ask yourself, "Is this something I would normally think, hear, or see? Is it something I would normally feel?" If the answer is no, then you are very likely having communication with someone outside of our reality! Discernment becomes easier with practice and, with wisdom, we never stop asking questions!

With time and practice, you will learn what actual communication feels like, and also learn to recognize when it is most likely something else. Along with becoming familiar and comfortable with paranormal communication, you also need to remain a little skeptical. It's healthy to question yourself to some extent. It's important to know that even though we are all intuitive in some way, we can make mistakes. We can misinterpret information. The best way to develop your gifts is to really get to know yourself, to work through any past issues so that you can become a clear channel. Once you do that, you are better able to discern real intuition from imagined.

Chapter 1
Developing Your Psychic Abilities

Example

I was once working at a psychic fair when I noticed that the psychic in the booth next to mine was telling every client the same thing; that their spouse was having an affair! Normally I tune out other people's readings, especially since I was busy giving readings. It did however strike me as odd. I know that infidelity happens, but not to everyone on the same day. Since I didn't know her very well and didn't feel comfortable talking with her about it, I went to the woman who was hosting the fair to express concern.

The host talked with the psychic privately and they decided she would leave the fair. I heard the psychic say to her, "You're right, I shouldn't have come today." She packed up her things and left.

After the fair was over I asked if she was okay. The hostess told me that she had received several complaints about her readings. Her clients felt that the information didn't ring true for them. In this case the clients were likely right. The psychic had found out the day before that her partner was having an affair.

She hadn't taken the time she needed to process what was happening in her life and to take care of her own emotional state. Bearing witness to her grief was an important lesson for me. The lesson here is to be aware of your own emotions and how they can affect your perceptions.

The Twelve Universal Laws

We are all, by default, working with Universal Law. After extensive research I have discovered that there are twelve Universal Laws that most people agree on. Thanks to some popular books and speakers over the years, most people are now familiar with the Law of Attraction. This is a Universal Law that is powerful all on its own, but combined with the other eleven laws, it becomes even more powerful and brings results much more quickly.

Remember that energy is neutral. It will respond to in kind to the energy you project. If you project frustration, you receive more things to be frustrated about. If you project doubtful feelings while thinking positively you will get mixed results because you are projecting two conflicting energies because the Universe automatically responds to both simultaneously. To achieve the results you want be in alignment with your thoughts, feelings and actions.

Your Spirit Guides can also complicate this process by interfering when what you want is not in your best interest. In this case you will usually get some kind of sign that your attempt won't work out the way you want it to. You will save yourself a lot of frustration by paying attention to the first sign you receive and adjusting your plan accordingly. In many cases a minor adjustment is all that's needed to get your manifesting moving again.

Chapter 1
Developing Your Psychic Abilities

Here is a brief introduction to the Twelve Universal Laws. As you are developing your intuitive skills, refer back to these laws to help you bypass some of the roadblocks that you may be putting in your own way.

- *The Law of Divine Oneness.* The crux of this law is that all things are connected. Every thought, feeling and action affects everything else.

- *The Law of Vibration.* Everything is made of energy and vibrates at its own rate. Each thought, feeling, idea, hope, disappointment, moment of anger has a vibration. You get to choose the vibration that supports your intuition. Remember, like attracts like vibrations.

- *The Law of Action.* Positive thinking and feeling are great and certainly clear the path for receiving, but until action is applied manifesting can fall flat. Practice using your intuition and you will accelerate faster than you imagined.

- *The Law of Correspondence.* Do what you feel and what you present to the world correspond? Making your insides match your outsides, taking control of your own life and leaving victimhood behind are the hallmarks of this law.

- *The Law of Cause and Effect.* Nothing happens by chance and every action has a reaction. Everything we do (Cause) has a consequence (Effect). We are responsible for our own lives based on the decisions we make and the actions we take.

- *The Law of Compensation*. This is similar to the Law of Cause and Effect, but dealing specifically with abundance and blessings. The concept of energy exchange is important to maintain balance in your relationships and within yourself. If you give, give, give and never receive any type of energy in exchange you will burn out and lose all interest in giving. Energy exchanges don't have to be monetary, they do have to be equitable.

- *The Law of Attraction*. Positive energy attracts more of the same. Negative energy attracts more of the same. This law is more about where your attention goes than what you actually want. We all want better, but if we are focused on the negative we will get more of that. For example, if you want more money to flow into your life, focus on receiving gifts of money, or a raise, rather on *needing* the money to pay bills. Focus on the joy of having rather than the lack of being in a state of needing.

- *The Law of Perpetual Transmutation of Energy*. You have the power to change any situation in your life! When you understand how the Universal Laws work, you can harness the positive energy to change the course of your life.

- *The Law of Relativity*. This law reminds you that you will have challenges that help you to grow spiritually, and so does everyone else. Whether you determine your challenges to be difficult or not is often based on how you see the challenges of another. Related to intuition, you may feel that your intuitive abilities are accurate or inaccurate based on the performance of your classmates.

- *The Law of Polarity*. All energies are on a continuum with its opposite. Fear and excitement are on opposite ends of the same energy line, perception is what determines the difference. This is also the case with darkness and light and positive and negative thoughts. The law highlights opposite ends of the same spectrum.

- *The Law of Rhythm*. Everything vibrates to its own rhythm. Whether or not you resonate with something or someone largely depends on how your vibrational frequency matches with the vibrational frequency of the person or thing you are in contact with.

- *The Law of Gender*. This could be more appropriately named the Law of Balance. In our dualistic world there is male and female energy. Ideally each person finds the balance within themselves, regardless of gender identity. Intuition is primarily considered to be a female trait, however as gender is becoming more fluid in society more people of all genders are embracing the power of their intuition.

As you can see by reading through these brief descriptions, many of the laws are similar. Understanding and application of the subtle differences is what will help you to delve deeply into your own intuition and make the most of it as you move forward.

Preparing Yourself for Intuitive Communication

Clearing and setting an energy space – why do it, what to use, and how to use it

Ideally, when you engage in any spiritual practice, you will have a clear "energy space" in which to do it. Wherever you are when you make a spiritual or metaphysical connection, you need to pay attention to how the environment feels. Is the energy around you light or heavy or somewhere in between? Having awareness of the energy in your environment gives you the opportunity to change that energy. Even if you aren't aware of how your immediate environment feels to you, you can still reset the energy to your liking. The following are some (not all) ways to intentionally change the energy in a space.

- Smudge the area with sage smoke or spray, incense, or any other scent that you prefer. Say a prayer or set your intention by saying which type(s) of energy you want to have in your space. Love, peace, and calm are examples of energy types you may want to invoke.

Chapter 1
Developing Your Psychic Abilities

- Light candles. You may light as many as you like and in any color you like. There are no absolute rules about this. When the candles are lit, follow the same instructions as you would for smudging.

- Use the violet light and white flame at the point in the room where the ceiling and the walls meet. Visualize the violet light like a neon tube of light going all the way around the perimeter of the room, then do the same with white light. For Reiki practitioners, the Reiki Symbols can be drawn on the ceiling, all four walls and the floor. If you like angels, ask angels to be in the corners of the room. Then follow the same instructions as you would for smudging.

- Another method of clearing and setting space is to use sound vibrations, whether in the form of singing bowls, recorded music, drums, or toning. Any sound that you find soothing or moving will work. And, of course, choose the energy you would like to have in your space.

As you can see, the methods you can use to change the energy in the space are varied and individual. Play with different ways to set your space and see what works for you.

Example for Clearing Energy

I was asked to clear a spirit from a home because the spirit was scaring the teenagers whose bedrooms were on the second floor of the house. From the moment I entered the building it was obvious to me that there was a lot of unsettled spirit energy in the house. There were no smokers living there and yet the entire place was filled with a haze. I could faintly hear all kinds of voices, but distant and muttering. There were far more spirits needing help than the homeowner realized. It was a new owner and they had just begun renovations on the older home, which can stir up any spirits who might be there...and there were a lot of them!

My preferred method of clearing in a situation like this is simple communication. So I started asking questions out loud to no one in particular, just to which ever spirits wanted to talk with me. One by one the started saying "I'm trapped". Then they started asking "why can't I leave?". It became almost deafening! This was happening on the first floor, I hadn't even reached the second floor yet. So, why are they all trapped here I wondered.

It then occurred to me to ask the homeowner about energetic protection on the home. Sure enough, a spiritual friend had placed a protection spell on the house because of the kids fearfulness. Also, she mentioned that a Native American Shaman had placed protection prior to her friend doing it. Oh, she had forgotten about the priest that the previous owner had brought in prior to the sale. Apparently the story goes that the priest left after placing his

Chapter 1
Developing Your Psychic Abilities

protection on the house, upset that it hadn't worked.

Interesting. I asked my guides what I should do to help these spirits. They suggested cutting a door through all of the layers of warding to give them the opportunity to leave. With my imaginary laser cutter I cut through all the layers of protective warding. There were actually four layers! Once the door was made the spirits started to leave, one after another they went through the door and directly into the light. All together 20 - 30 spirits left the house in less than a minute. I then put a temporary cover on the door way, incase we needed it again I didn't want to seal it up completely just yet.

Almost instantly the haze cleared, we could physically see better! That was the first time I remember seeing a physical result so clearly.

Now it was time to go upstairs to see what was going on up there. As I climbed the stairs I felt more sad and frightened with each step. When we reached the top of the stairs, the homeowner told me that the kids were afraid of "the scary old man" who was always in their rooms. It didn't take long for me to see him standing by the window looking out. He looked sad. I asked him if I could help, his response was that no one could. He didn't know what he had done wrong to be kept prisoner, but he was pretty sure that I couldn't help him. He was so frightened that this was going to be his eternal home.

I asked him how he got there, in that house. He told me that he and his wife had the house built when they were first married.

They loved it and raised their family in that house. After she passed he lived there until he passed. Then the kids sold the house to someone who rented it out to other people. But he could never leave, try as he might. His wife got to go to heaven, why didn't he? This poor man was shrouded in sadness and fear.

At this point I told him about the layers of protection on the house and the door that I had opened downstairs, and that I could make a door for him as well. He brightened a little, but was skeptical, not believing he would be allowed to go to heaven. I wondered what it would take to convince him. His response was "if Christ himself comes to get me!"! Um, okay. I suggested that we ask, the worst that could happen is that the answer is no. So I cut a door into the layers of warding and asked Christ to help this man to be released from this home that he had been trapped inside. Of course his request was answered, Christ came right into the room and took his hand as they floated off together into the Light.

My guides then instructed me to remove all of the layers of protection that had been applied to the house and property while they swept through the house to make sure all of the trapped that may have missed the first door were able to leave before we applied a new protective layer to replace the others. One guardian spirit chose to stay behind.

The moral of the story is, be sure to clear a space BEFORE setting a space. You don't want to accidentally trap anyone inside.

Chapter 1
Developing Your Psychic Abilities

Example for Setting Energy

Years ago I was selling insurance for a living. Not just insurance, but high risk business and agricultural insurance. It was a low vibration job for a low vibration company, a job I didn't keep for very long. While I was there, however, I did my best to keep my own office's vibration high.

Every day I went to work I set a vibrational space in my office using the Violet Light and White flame method. I set the space with intention for honesty, integrity, compassion, wisdom and prosperity. Only honest people with integrity were allowed to enter my office!

One morning, my boss, holding a policy in a folder, was looking down at the papers in his hands as he attempted to walk into my office. He literally bounced off of the protection that I had set even though the physical door to my office was open. He looked up, surprised that something had stopped him from entering the room. He took a step back, looked at the open door and tried again. Again he bounced off of the energetic forcefield. He was a man lacking in integrity and compassion, therefore he was not allowed to enter in the space I had set.

When you practice working with energy, the results can be amazingly powerful!

Personal Energy Awareness

Why it's necessary and how to become aware. Some call this "self protection."

It's in your best interest to be aware of the energy around you all the time. In order to be aware of the energy around you, you first need to be aware of your *own* energy. Once you consciously know what your own energy feels like, you automatically become aware when the energy outside your personal space changes, whether it feels comfortable or feels uncomfortable.

When you learn to think in terms of "all is energy", you become less afraid and simply understand that if you are uncomfortable in any place or situation, it's because the energy in that place or situation does not resonate with you. Awareness of your own energy field alerts you to those changes and allows you to deal with all situations with less panic, fear, or judgment.

When you are unaware of your own energy, specifically how far away from your body your energy spreads, you can find yourself exhausted, angry without knowing why, or feeling drained. Since most of you have not been taught to manage your energy, you often have a large field through which many other energies can move. Every time that happens, you are affected without even knowing it. So how do you manage your energy fields? You think about it; that's the key! With the power of your own mind, you

Chapter 1
Developing Your Psychic Abilities

can visualize exactly how far away from your body want your energy field to be. Just close your eyes and visualize drawing your energy to you. You can see it as light, as a shrinking bubble that gets smaller the closer it gets to you, or in any other way that works for you.

Eighteen to twenty-four inches is a pretty good distance for your energy field to be from your body. That's a fairly comfortable conversational distance, allowing only those whom you want into your personal space. Your instructor will help you see how large your personal energy field is by using dowsing rods or a to show you just how far away from your body that your energy is. Once you learn to control your own energy field, you can make conscious choices regarding how large or small you want yours to be.

Personal Energy Exercise

Have a friend stand about twenty feet from you. Your friend should be holding a pendulum or divining rods in front of them facing you. When they are holding it so that it isn't moving, start walking toward that person until the pendulum or divining rods move on their own. When that happens stop walking. Whatever the distance between you and the other person, that's the distance that your personal energy field is extending out from you, all the way around you in all directions.

If the distance between you and the divining rods is more than twenty four

> *inches, return to your previous position, pull your energy in again give it another try. You can practice as much as needed until you feel you can control your energy field.*

Centering and Grounding

What it is, why it's necessary and how to do it.

Centering is feeling at peace, knowing who you are (at least in the moment). It's a sense that all is well, like you can handle anything, and do so with ease and grace. It's gratitude for all that you have and all that you are. Being centered gives you a sense of confidence because you know that all is One and you are never alone. It is a comfort level with who you are and what you are about and often involves a feeling of love and a general sense of well-being.

Grounding is knowing that your spirit is as fully in your body as possible. When you're grounded, you can think more clearly and have an easier time concentrating. You also get more accomplished in the physical world when grounded. Being grounded helps you to be clear in understanding your life's purpose and makes it easier to understand how to honor that purpose. Being grounded when you perform spiritual work allows you to convey messages with greater clarity.

Ideally, you are centered and grounded at the same time, allowing you to easily tap into the intuition that will help you receive and make sense of messages in the here and now. When you are both centered and

Chapter 1
Developing Your Psychic Abilities

balanced, it's much easier to receive messages that are clear to both you and your client.

> *All energy work, whether psychic or healing, should always start with a prayer or intention for the highest good of everyone involved.*

You may not always know what the highest good is for everyone who may be affected by the energy work you do. You may not even be aware of how many people could be affected, especially by the information that comes through during a reading. You also have no control over what people *hear* regardless of what you actually *say*. You may have set *your filters* aside, and that doesn't mean that the person receiving the reading has set *their filters* aside. They are still going to hear what you say through *their filters,* which is likely to skew the information you give them regardless of how clearly your explain the message.

For these reasons, it iss in your best interest to ask for Divine Universal help, whatever that means for you. Setting your space using one of the methods we've already discussed is a great first step. For each person with whom you work it's a good idea to set the intention that they receive exactly what they are meant to receive during the reading.

Divination Tools

Intuitives have used many different tools throughout history to aid them in receiving and understanding messages from beyond the physical plane. The Oracles at Delphi used gaseous vapors from a volcano. Shamans from all over the world use a deep meditation called a "journey" to the upper, middle, and lower worlds to "gather" information for themselves and others. Tea leaves, crystal balls, smoke from a fire, a single flame from a candle, are just a few of the many examples I could cite here. For the sake of this class, we will discuss and practice with the divination tools most commonly used in our culture today.

Your own intuition is your greatest divination tool. No matter which other tools you use, they only help you clarify the information you receive intuitively. With time and practice, you may realize that it's the only tool you need. As you learn to trust yourself to interpret the messages you are receiving, you will begin to understand that it doesn't even matter which, if any, other tools you use.

Pendulums are one way of getting quick answers to questions, usually of the yes/no variety. They are often used in energy healing to identify energy blockages so that the healer can address specific problems more quickly. You can also use pendulums to see if your chakras are closed or blocked.

Although many pendulums have crystals and other stones on them, they don't have to.

Chapter 1

Developing Your Psychic Abilities

Any object that can freely swing on a 4 - 6 inch string or chain can be used as a pendulum. What matters is the intention with which you use it and that it resonates with you. Many metaphysical/spiritual stores carry pendulums both online and onsite. Sometimes local artisans who make beaded or stone jewelry will have pendulums available for purchase. You can also make your own if you are inclined to do so. As a general rule pendulums are fairly inexpensive.

They can be used with a "pendulum board" or by themselves. You can purchase a pendulum board or make your own. Pre-made boards usually look something like this;

You can easily make your own pendulum board with any piece of paper and a pen. When making your own board you can make it specific to a question, for example, "where would I be most happy living?" Draw a half circle and write down all of the places you are thinking about moving to along the curved part of the half circle. Then hold the pendulum over the center of the line at the bottom of the half circle and ask your question.

To get the best result from your pendulum, prepare for communication as we discussed earlier. Ask your guides, Higher Power, angels…whomever you are in contact with, to move the pendulum to honestly answer your questions. Beware of asking the same question in multiple ways. If you do so and the answer changes, then you have taken control of the energy of the pendulum and are no longer receiving guidance from a higher source.

Also, to receive clear, truthful information it's best to not be emotionally invested in the outcome of a pendulum reading. When emotionally invested, you can easily create a false reading from the pendulum by influencing it to give you the answer you prefer.

Divining rods, sometimes called *dowsing rods* are similar to pendulums in that they move in response to energy. Divining rods, Y shaped branches, and pendulums have been used for thousands of years to find all sorts of things, most notably underground freshwater sources. They have also been used to find mineral deposits and even missing people and pets. For the purpose of this class, we use them to help define the edge of your personal energy field to help you learn to control your own energy. (Refer to the exercise in Chapter 1.)

Chapter 1
Developing Your Psychic Abilities

Probably the most common tools being used today for divination are cards. *Tarot, oracle, and angel cards* are available almost everywhere and come in hundreds of different varieties. They can be found online at retailers like amazon.com and eBay as well as on the websites of independently owned metaphysical stores. If you prefer the personal touch of in-store shopping, most bookstores and independently owned metaphysical/spiritual stores will likely have at least some decks in stock. Your instructor should be able to direct you to local outlets where card decks are available.

When choosing a deck for your own personal use, be sure the energy of the deck and the artwork resonate with you. Most card decks come with instructions, which include the author's intended meaning for each of the cards. We encourage you to use the book that comes with the card deck as little as possible. This class is designed to help you tap into and increase your intuition.If you memorize a book, you will bypass your intuition. You will have the opportunity to do your first tarot, or angel card reading at the beginning of Chapter Two. Your instructor should have cards available that you can use. You are also welcome to bring your own deck if you prefer.

Again, there are many, many tools you can use to enhance your intuition. Just a few are listed here. As you continue on your own spiritual and self-ascension path, you will discover which tools resonate with you. You are also likely to discover many more tools not mentioned here, or to create your own.

During the course of this program, I encourage you to practice what you read in each chapter before moving on to the next. At the end of each chapter, you will find suggested activities to help you use what you are learning.

Practice activities for Chapter One

- *Meditate daily keeping a journal of impressions, feelings, visions, dreams, etc.*
- *Choose a tool to practice with and practice as often as possible with it and journal your results.*

Chapter 1 Notes
_____
_____
_____
_____
_____
_____
_____

Chapter 1
Developing Your Psychic Abilities

Chapter 2: Discerning Energy and Intuition

Now that you've had exposure to some of the tools intuitive readers use, think about what worked and what didn't.
- *How did each of the tools work for you?*
- *Which did you like best, and why?*

Your Notes
_____
_____
_____
_____
_____
_____
_____
_____
_____
_____
_____
_____

Chapter 2
Discerning Energy and Intuition

Keep in mind that these tools work differently for every person. My reason for introducing you to several different tools is so you can try them out and decide which tools, if any, resonate with you. Remember that regardless of which tools you choose to use or not to use, your most important resource is your awareness of your own energy field. As long as you are controlling your own energy, you can connect and disconnect to or from anyone at any time your choose. A precautionary warning, only connect to people who have given you permission to do so. Connecting to someone else without permission is an invasion of privacy and ethically frowned upon.

Cards

The next tool for you to try is the cards. Tarot, oracle, animal totems, angels...that's up to you. Oracle cards of all types are generally fairly self explanatory, so let's focus on reading with tarot cards. Tarot decks are available in hundreds of styles. What they have in common is that each one has 78 cards.The deck is split into two main categories, the Major Arcana and the Minor Arcana.

The Major Arcana has 22 cards, collectively known as "The Fool's Journey," and usually start with the fool as number zero. Note that different decks may call the cards different names. For example in the Sacred Circle Tarot Deck the fool is called the green man. The fool is inexperienced; new to everything. The Fool's Journey represents our journey through life, with all of its joys, sorrows and lessons. The Major Arcana is for contemplation and learning.

The Minor Arcana is modeled after playing cards. It has four suits, each with 14 cards, starting with the Ace and ending with the King. Most decks have Swords, Cups, Staffs (sometimes called Wands or Staves) and Coins (sometimes called Pentacles, Sacred Circles or Discs). Overall the Minor Arcana indicates actions for you to take in your life.

There is no need to memorize the "meaning" of each individual card, although it is helpful to understand what each suit represents. Swords represent intellect, reason, thinking. Cups are interpreted as emotions, flow, dealing with relationships. Staves have to do with our purpose, life path, why we are here, how to move forward with understanding, and act on our purpose. Coins deal with money and other earthly concerns. Although this is generally how the suits are labeled, keep in mind that different authors may change the meaning of each suit for their own deck. Use your own discernment and intuition in choosing how you will interpret the meanings of suits and individual cards in your readings.

It's a good idea when you first get a deck of cards to spend some time looking at the cards, getting a feel for them. Move them around in your hands or shuffle them gently if you like. Meditate with them, putting your energy into them before you even do a first

Chapter 2
Discerning Energy and Intuition

reading for yourself or anyone else.

When you begin to practice reading cards, start with something simple. A good way to familiarize yourself with a new deck is to choose one card per day and study it. You may wish to ask a question, aloud or silently, before choosing a card from the deck. You may choose a card by spreading the cards out face down on a table and "feeling" for a card to answer your question by slowly waving your hand above the cards until your hand moves over a card that "feels right." Turn that card over and study the image on it to discern the answer to your question.

To discern the message the card is relaying to you, be aware of whatever draws your attention first. Think of a question and then look at the card below.

This 9 of Wands card was randomly chosen from The Sacred Circle Tarot deck. When you look at the card, what is the first thing you notice? Is it the fire encircling the card? The Celtic Knots in all four corners? Maybe it's the green valley or the grey sky. Did you first notice the grid in front made of wands? Was it the word "Recovery" at the top of the card? Whatever it was, what did it mean to you? How does it answer your question? Once you have practiced with your cards, you may want to offer a practice reading to a friend who will give you honest feedback.

Now that you've done a practice tarot reading with a friend, you have probably noticed that some of the answers don't come automatically or easily. Relax, it's ok. For many of you, this is your first experience divining answers in this way. It will get easier with practice. The more you practice any skill, the more comfortable you become with it. Here are some suggestions to keep your brain from stopping intuitive messages as you practice with your cards.

As with any skill you work to develop, success in reading cards comes down to awareness. If you don't know "how" the communication is being blocked, you won't know what to do to unblock it. Be patient with yourself, the more you intentionally work with spiritual energy, the easier it will get for you receive communications.

Chapter 2
Discerning Energy and Intuition

How to Deal with Being Blocked

Here are some examples of how you can be blocked and what to do about it.

Thinking about what to say

Learn to recognize when you are trying to think of what to say. If you are working to think of something to say, you will get caught up in the *thinking* and be unable to just allow the information to come **through** you. Take a deep breath and relax. Visualize setting your mind (or you may call it ego, if you prefer) aside to get it out of the way of your intuition.

- First, visualize your mind/ego as an object, like a crystal. Some people see their mind/ego as an animal, like a lion. Regardless of how you see it, you must set it aside.

- The second step is to create a visualization to set your mind/ego. Remember that you are dealing with a part of you, so be gentle and respectful with your mind/ego. You will need it back when you are finished with your intuitive exercise. For example, if you visualize it as a large crystal, your next step is to create a nice safe place to keep it. A cushioned container would be a nice choice. A more clear example would be an ornately carved box with a cushion inside that perfectly fits the crystal.

- Step three is to close the box and set it aside. Once you've done this, you are free to open completely to the flow of intuition.

Body Sensations

Pay attention to body sensations (without getting stuck on what you are paying attention to), cold chills or sudden extreme heat, for example on your arm, can be an indication of an energy shift in the room. Tingling sensations or goose bumps are generally accepted as an awareness of paranormal energy. Once you are aware of the energy, start asking questions aloud or silently to see if you can get more information about the energy. For instance, you can ask if the energy you feel is a spirit guide, angel, or someone who is trying to talk with someone who is still here. You can ask if the energy has any messages to pass along or ask it questions about itself, like has it ever lived on Earth. Get creative and ask whatever questions come to you.

Expectations about Messages

Expecting the messages you receive to come to you in a certain way will prevent you from recognizing the messages you do receive. We often expect that intuitive messages will be profoundly obvious when the truth is that they are often very subtle. Pay attention to the small things that may seem insignificant - they usually contain the information that you need. We often look so hard for the burning bush that we miss the brief spark. What seems like a passing thought or a feeling that comes and goes quickly can be significant to the other person. Also, if a thought keeps coming back to you, say it no matter how weird it may seem. Very

Chapter 2
Discerning Energy and Intuition

likely it will make complete sense to the other person. As an example, "fuzzy pink bunny slippers" could keep coming to mind and make no sense to you at all, but maybe the person you are reading was given a pair of them by their grandmother. It could very well be communication from that person's grandmother.

Example

A young man came to me for a reading after his grandfather passed away. He was distraught that his grandfather hadn't left any mementos for him like he had for some others. During the reading, his grandfather spoke to me giving me the exact location of a wooden box he intended for his grandson. The grandfather both explained to me verbally and showed me a "picture" of the exact location of the box. He also described in great detail.

A few weeks later the young man called to tell me that the box was exactly where his grandfather said it would be! And, it was filled with memories that the two of them had made together, including pictures, fishing lures and tickets to ball games.

Example

A middle aged woman wearing a business suit came to me for a reading shortly after the loss of her mother. She had practical questions about paperwork and how she hid her illness from the family, but all her mother kept showing me was a baseball.

The daughter was clearly frustrated and looking for the answers SHE wanted. The mother was not in the least interested in any of that stuff and only kept showing me the baseball. We were obviously getting nowhere.

Up to this point I was only asking the mother the questions that the daughter wanted answers to and hadn't mentioned the baseball. But mom wasn't giving up!

At this point I'm pretty sure the daughter was convinced that I had no idea what I was doing. So I finally said "Look, she's showing me a baseball. She doesn't want to talk about anything else until I tell you about the baseball. For some reason it's really important to her." The daughter gasped and smiled through her tears as she told me that in her youth, her mother played on an all girls professional baseball team and that her mother had taught her how to play baseball as a child.

Once that connection was made, the rest of the reading resulted in the woman getting the answers she was looking for.

Chapter 2
Discerning Energy and Intuition

Discerning Energy Types

Energy is what everything is made of, from the air around us to your kitchen table. It's all made of energetic components. Just like everything else we are made of energy, too. This is true whether or not we currently possess a physical body. Without passing judgment as to whether energy is "good" or "bad," you need to know how people understand the different forms energy can take in order to correctly understand the messages that you are getting.

Remember - we are all made of energy, which means disembodied energy and the energy in a physical body can both vibrate at varying speeds. The faster energy vibrates, the more light it produces. Energy with a fast vibration is considered to be "higher" energy. Think about the people you know. Some people are just brighter and vibrate at a high level, while others feel heavy. People who feel heavy have a hard time emanating light from themselves, which means others often perceive them as being "dark" or "mean." The truth is they are vibrating at a lower level, more slowly, than their "brighter" counterparts.

Ghosts

Lower corporeal energies, most commonly called "ghosts," are energies that are no longer in bodies but are still on the Earth plane. Some stay because they don't know that they can move on. Some don't even realize that they have left their bodies, which seems to happen mostly when "death" is quick and unexpected. And, as you will discover, some energies that are bound to the Earth are kept here purely by the thoughts and behaviors of those still "living."

Example

During a third home energy cleansing on the same place within a year's time, I saw some patterns emerging. Dark blobs of energy appeared every time. They didn't have a human-like form, they were just black blobs. The blobs felt heavy and had an element of residual anger to them, just like the first two times I did cleansings on this house. Each time I cleansed the energy from the house, it returned in a few months. I knew something was off, that something was drawing the energy back there, or recreating it. The owner declined a reading when it was offered, so I just did the job and left.

The difference the third time was that the homeowner didn't clean his house before I arrived like he had previously. Now I was able to see ALL of the reasons that the dark energy kept returning. There was evidence of gambling, drug use, and bizarre stuff I won't even mention here. The homeowner kept creating situations that invited that sort of energy. This time he inquired as to why the dark energy kept returning. After I did the cleansing, I answered his question. He didn't like the answer and I never heard from him again.

Chapter 2
Discerning Energy and Intuition

Some ghosts stay by choice, either to guide and help others or because they don't want to leave. Some cross over to the Light and then return because they want to. Although they are still considered to be "ghosts," these energies vibrate at a "higher" level than those who are "stuck."

The two most important things to remember when dealing with energy are that there are no absolutes and that things are rarely as they appear. Our general understanding of physics simply doesn't apply to anything beyond our physical world, and a great deal of how we process any information is based on our understanding of physics. Outside of our physical world, time and space are irrelevant. Once someone leaves our physical world, their "personality" as we knew it begins to fade. However, they can recapture or recreate it in order to convey messages to us.

How Energy Appears

As you can see, metaphysics is not as simple as it may seem. Let's discuss some of the ways energy can appear. For reasons of simplicity, we will discuss energy in three different ways. Although energy can manifest in many ways, we will start with these three.

Keep in mind as we go through these different perceptions of energy that they are "*perceptions*." Perception is how the mind understands incoming information. We decide if information is "true" or "false" based on our understanding of that information *after* it has been through our *filters*. Basically, how we *feel* about any particular piece of information determines whether we believe it to be "true" or not.

Resonant Energy

When something resonates with us, we believe it to be true. We *know* it to be true. It feels right, it just fits. This is called *Resonant Energy*. Resonant energy often comes with confirmation, or a signal that you interpret as something being true. Confirmation can come from someone for whom you are doing an intuitive reading when it also resonates with them. It can come in the form of "goosebumps" or chills, a sudden warm spot on a specific part of your body, like your arm or your ears. You may sense you are being watched. It's a "knowing" that you feel deeply within yourself and for which you have no other explanation to offer.

Self or Mind-Created Energy Interpretation

We are all very powerful creative beings, and most of us can convince ourselves of anything! For this reason, we need to be careful of creating stories around energy, and believing them. Although energy cannot be created or destroyed, it can be misinterpreted and misunderstood. Energy can also be

Chapter 2
Discerning Energy and Intuition

manipulated. When you misinterpret energy, you can trick yourself into believing that you feel something that simply isn't so. This is *Self or Mind Created Energy Interpretation.* This is the energy you *think* you are feeling rather than the energy that is actually present. Likewise you can allow yourself *not* to feel the energy that *is* actually present. (Aren't we just tricky?)

Several situations could lend themselves to the manifestation of this phenomena. As humans we are all susceptible to the suggestion, this is one way we misinterpret energy and convince ourselves what we are experiencing is real. The best way to prevent this from happening is to really get to know yourself and to have confidence in that knowledge and in your intuitive abilities. By knowing your own truths, and trusting in your abilities to receive and interpret messages intuitively, your understanding cannot be influenced by someone else's opinion.

Along the same lines, when you are confident in your ability to interpret messages, you will be less likely to change your interpretations to fulfill the wishes of the person for who you are doing a reading.. It's natural to want others to be happy, especially when their momentary happiness seems to hinge on the information you are giving. This is where you need to be careful not to skew the information. It's important to remain honest with people even if it isn't what they want to hear at that moment. In the end your honesty will serve them, and it will serve you.

Similar to the power of suggestion, mass hysteria has a way of overruling an individual's intuition. It's easy to get caught up in the energy created when a group of people get excited (or frightened) and to ignore any intuitive information that may be coming to you. Do your best not to get carried away with the group energy, staying as centered and grounded as you can in order to remain in touch with your own intuition. Just remember that it may require you to move away from the crowd in order to get clear.

(Note: *Lack of awareness regarding your own moral or political filters is yet another way that you may allow your own "self created energy" to skew what you experience. We will cover this in greater detail in Chapter Three.)

Deceptive Energy

As a reminder - we are powerful creative beings. If we aren't careful, we can use those powers of creation to deceive ourselves. We can miss cues that something isn't quite right. Sometimes we do it out of fear, reading danger or suffering into situations where it doesn't actually exist. Sometimes it's just the opposite. The importance of remaining mindful that a "story" or situation can present itself in a *Deceptive* way cannot be overstated.

"*Deceptive Energy*" is energy that can appear different than it actually is. We must

Chapter 2
Discerning Energy and Intuition

be sure that we are clear ourselves before entering into a situation that may be misleading. A "situation" can be anything from doing a reading or energy healing to clearing and blessing a home or business. The more clear you are when you start, the less likely you will be deceived. When you are clear, you enter into these situations without expectations or judgment about what the energy is. Only with clarity can you see anything the way it truly is.

Your own perceptions likely deceive you more than anything else. For example, if you perceive the world as broken and needing to be fixed, then you will deceive yourself into believing that every energy you come into contact is either "broken" and in need of mending or is the "breaker" and needs to be eliminated. This particular perception also qualifies as a filter, which we will discuss later. What if neither of these scenarios is true?

Most often what we judge as "good" or "bad' energy is actually our perception of the frequency at which that energy is vibrating. We, as humans, tend to experience lower frequency energy as negative and then formulate ideas to reinforce our understanding of what "negative" means. Unfortunately, we do ourselves and others a great disservice when we process the information in this way. If we learn to think of energy as a neutral building block of the Universe, then we can remove judgment and be more effective in consciously working with energy. By removing judgment, seeing the energy more clearly, and remaining open to guidance, you will be better able to understand how to work with energy to help others; whether the "others" are in or out of bodies.

"Attachments" are another way that *Deceptive Energy* can present itself. In this case, attachment is "a negative corporeal entity that is attached to a living human being." In the realm of Spirituality, disembodied energy *can* attach to a physical person, but it rarely does. More often than not, it's exactly the opposite. Fear can be a powerful force in creating more fear, and the mind of someone who doesn't understand how manifestation works can easily feel an attachment and not realize they created it themselves.

Grief can do the same thing. When you grieve the loss of a loved one, you can hold the energy of that person to the Earth plane, at least for a while, and sometimes indefinitely.

A few more things to keep in mind as you begin to do intuitive readings

When giving or receiving an intuitive reading, it may be helpful to know what a reading is supposed to be. Readings are intended to provide guidance for the living in a conscious way. The following guidelines may be helpful as you learn and practice using your intuition.

Chapter 2

Discerning Energy and Intuition

Before you begin an intuitive reading, make sure to set your space using the techniques in Chapter One.

- Center and balance yourself with a brief meditation so that you are calm and feel connected to Spirit.

- When you have done that, focus your attention to your heart center and envision it opening to send a stream of energy to the heart center of the person you are reading, connecting with that person so that you are able to feel or experience from his/her perspective.

- It can also be helpful to consciously connect your third eye or crown directly to the Universe. This second connection point can open a more clear channel for you receive information intuitively.

- Once you feel that you are connected, you probably begin by asking your client if they have any questions, unless you are already receiving information for them. If you are already receiving information for them, state the thoughts, images, feelings, and/or or what you are hearing in a clear and understandable way. If your client doesn't have a question, then your question to Spirit/The Universe becomes "What does _____ need to know at this time?".

Often, when someone seeks out an Intuitive Reading it's because he or she is experiencing confusion or emotional pain and is looking for guidance, clarity or confirmation. There are times when a person may just need someone to talk to, and they choose you. Very often a reading is more listening than talking. Do your best to listen carefully to discern what it is the person actually needs. When you have a clearer understanding of the need, ask your Guides (or whomever you work with) to help you help them. Then share with compassion, understanding and empathy any information that comes to you. Always be as honest and as gentle as possible. Brutal honesty will only serve to shut down most people's emotions and prevent them from getting what they need from the reading.

Some precautions to take when doing intuitive readings

Be careful not to point out the obvious or what you believe to be "common sense" unless you specifically say that's what you are doing. Sometimes, in the course of clarifying why a person wants a reading, you may find yourself having a conversation involving a verbal "wading through" of the person's thought process. When you are more clear as to their need, go ahead with the intuitive reading.

Remember that when you are doing an intuitive reading, your opinions, viewpoints,

Chapter 2
Discerning Energy and Intuition

and beliefs have no bearing on the reading. Everyone is, of course, entitled to have these things. No one, however, is entitled to push their personal opinions, viewpoints, or beliefs onto someone else. You need to set aside your opinions and beliefs when you set aside the mind/ego. This can sometimes be difficult, especially if you feel strongly about a particular topic. If someone comes to you asking for a reading that involves a topic you feel you can not be objective about, it's in everyone's best interest to refer them to another reader. This will be covered in more depth in Chapter Three.

Intuitive readings can be incredibly therapeutic. Often the information that comes through can help to guide the receiver of the reading in making decisions with more clarity, help someone through the grieving process after the loss of a loved one or to aid them in understanding their own Spiritual gifts. At times it can be helpful for you as the reader to share an appropriate part of your own story to help your clients better understand the message. Be conservative in how much you share with the client. Keep the focus on them.

The job of any Intuitive is ultimately to help people. Good readings can literally change lives by helping people realize how empowered they really are. This is why it's so very important for you to remember that you should never tell the client what to do or how to do it. As Intuitive Readers, we simply share our impressions and leave all decisions up to the recipient. Explain the information that you receive more deeply if need be, just don't make any decisions for anyone else. Leading people to their own self empowerment is hallmark of a really good Psychic.

Practice activities for Chapter Two

- *Continue journalling your meditative experiences and dreams.*
- *Continue to work with different tools or refining your intuition without the use of tools.*

Chapter Two Notes

_____
_____
_____
_____
_____
_____
_____
_____
_____
_____

Chapter 2
Discerning Energy and Intuition

Chapter 3: Mediumship

Now that you've learned how to set a space, ground and center yourself, connect with another person, and the dos and don'ts of doing a reading, it's time to practice doing a one-on-one reading. You will need someone to practice with. Ideally the person you choose will be supportive of what you are doing, and also honest with you. You will give that person a reading using any tool of divination that you like, including your own intuition without the aid of another tool. When you are finished, ask for honest feedback about the quality of the reading you gave. Remember that this is just practice, and that you are just learning. Be kind to yourself and learn from the feedback, particularly what they liked and what you could improve upon.

Preparing for Paranormal Communication: Mediumship

Mediumship, in the simplest of terms, is communicating with those who have left our physical world. It's a very specific type of reading and usually has a very specific focus; to talk to someone "on the other side." This is different than a general intuitive reading where the focus is on gathering information without specific regard to the source of the information.

Chapter 3
Mediumship

Contact can be made either from our physical plane or from the spiritual plane. Sometimes when you are contacted from the other side, it is called a haunting. There are several types of "hauntings," which we will cover in Chapter Five. Other times, you call it being contacted by loved ones. Either way, we label the experience based on whether or not we knew the person and how we perceive the experience. Contacts from the spirit world can happen at any time and without warning. These contacts can leave those who were visited feeling anything from terrified to loved and happy.

For the purpose of this book (and class), we will focus on how you can initiate communication. To start, prepare your space with light, sage, or incense, and the intention of your communication. Always remember to only invite in those of the **Highest Order of Love and Light**. Center and ground yourself by meditating and quieting your mind. When you are ready you can begin to invoke communication by inviting spirits to participate in discussion with you.

The questions you ask when extending the invitation for communication will vary depending on why you are inviting communication. For example, if a woman named "Jane" came to you asking if any of her family on the other side are with her, you would likely ask something like "Does anyone want to talk with, or have any messages for Jane?" Then remain quiet for a few moments while you "listen" for an answer. The answer may come in any of the ways we discussed in Chapter One. Pay attention to the subtleties of thought, vision, smells, and other sensations. If you get a sense of someone, describe what you sense to your client to see if she can confirm the information for you.

Here's another scenario to consider. A client comes to you hoping to speak with her mother, whose name is Edith. In this case, you would ask something like, "Edith, Jane would like to talk with you, are you here?" Then wait again for a moment to see if you get anything. Whatever you get, share it. See if the other person can confirm the information for you. By the way, it's fine to ask the client for the name of the person they are hoping to contact. Not everyone can easily "hear" names, and it's better to just ask up front rather than to guess incorrectly and put your perceived legitimacy in question.

Receiving and Interpreting Messages

When receiving information through intuition, it's natural to question your ability to accurately interpret the messages. After all, nobody is 100% right 100% of the time. You might as well make peace with it now, and cut yourself and everyone else some slack. A number of factors can affect how well you receive and interpret information, some within your control and some not within your control.

Chapter 3
Mediumship

Factors Out of Your Control

Beginning with what is *not* in your control, let's take a look at some factors that may make receiving and interpreting messages more difficult.

Illness

When you are physically not feeling well you will want to reconsider doing readings for anyone. It can take a lot of energy to connect with and then disconnect from people, and when you don't feel well expending the extra energy may be too draining. This applies to everything from a headache or cold to a bad day with a chronic condition or menstrual cramps. Pain is distracting and can prevent you from making contact with those beyond, or it can skew the information because we all tend to lean a little more toward the negative when we are in pain. Also, if there is a chance that you may be contagious, please be courteous and stay away from people until you are better. Thanks, we all appreciate it!

Life Events

Things happen in life, and we are affected. It's perfectly human. We are, overall, a pretty sensitive lot and that sensitivity needs to be honored. So when something truly upsetting happens in your life, that's not the time to be doing readings for other people. If you have recently had a loved one, whether family, friend or pet, cross over into Spirit, take the time to grieve and take care of yourself. This is not the time to push your feelings down and "be a trooper." If you wouldn't advise someone else to do it, follow that advice for yourself.

Relationships

There are also times when those you love may do hurtful things and you are affected by those behaviors. Again, this is out of your control, but you may still be in an emotional state which would prevent you from receiving and interpreting messages clearly. For example if an Intuitive Reader found out only a few hours prior to doing a reading that her life partner had been having an affair, she would not be in the proper state of mind (or emotion) to guide anyone, especially if the client was asking about relationship issues. These are, of course, only two examples. Knowing yourself well enough to know when NOT to do Intuitive/Energetic work is just as important as knowing how to do it. Respecting your humanness and limitations is paramount to your Intuitive success.

Factors In Your Control

A great many factors are, however, within your control. The way that you manage daily stress, your diet and exercise, how hard you push yourself and more are certainly within your control.

Chapter 3
Mediumship

Self care is an absolute must for anyone working with Spiritual Energy

---

The most important strength each of us has is power over our own attitude. The more we live in gratitude the happier we are and the more open we are to our own intuition. When we are focusing more on worry and fear than on love and gratitude, we may still be open to receiving, but we are also more likely to interpret incoming information in negative ways. The choice is always available to us.

Feeling Blocked? Tips for Getting Past the Blocks

Relax. The more relaxed you are, the more confidence you will have. You will also appear to be more confident to the recipient of your reading, and to any spirits who are coming to you. If you allow yourself to get frustrated, you will be less likely to experience any communication that comes to you. Take a deep breath, release it, and invite conversation like you learned in Chapter Two. Let it come naturally, and it usually will.

The fear of being wrong or looking incompetent can be pretty strong. No one wants to put themselves out there and risk looking foolish. For that reason, even seasoned professionals sometimes hold back information that may appear to be nonsense, don't. If you get a message, convey it. even if it sounds crazy or doesn't seem to make sense, it will likely make sense to your client. Often when the message is obscure, it's directed right to the person who's meant to have it. As an example, if you are checking to see if anyone on the other side has a message for your client and all you are getting is an image of a fish, that isn't likely to make any sense to you at all. Say it anyway. It could be that your client went fishing with a grandfather when he was a kid and caught his first fish. That fish might be the one thing bringing the connection together, but you won't know until you say something.

If the message you receive is for you and it doesn't seem to make sense, you can ask for clarification. More often than most of us would prefer, the spirit world can be cryptic, and it can drive us crazy! When it comes to mediumship we need to remember that our loved ones changed when they entered the world of Spirit. At the moment of "death" consciousness expands. The limits of being human lift, the person has a greater comprehension of all of the things we still don't fully understand in our human form. When they try to share this knowledge, it's beyond us. We just don't get it. We are even more confused by the cryptic messages because we generally don't understand that they are no longer just the person we knew, they are more. Be patient, the meaning or significance may come to you later.

If a message comes through for you in the

Chapter 3
Mediumship

midst of reading for someone else, make a mental note of it and return to that message at another time. Your loved one will understand.

Remember that when you are working with the other side, or with your guides or your angels, that you are a member of the team that is getting the message through to someone on this side. We need them to give us the messages and they need us to relay them. This is an important point to remember. *We are not puppets for the spirit realm.* Set boundaries. Sometimes you will not be available to take messages, like when you're driving or at work. Ask whomever is giving you the message to come back at a time when you're available and make sure you tell them when that time is, like after dinner or at bedtime. There is no "time" in the spirit world, so using a clock time, like 9:30, will most likely not work. Instead, make the contact based on energy or activity.

When interpreting a message it's important to remember we all have our own filters. Everything that we experience is run through those filters and determines how we understand what is happening. Mental and emotional filters are created by many factors, here are some of the most common contributing factors:

- Religious beliefs, even those we no longer adhere to, can leave an imprint on our thought process and value systems.

- Anything that we feel strongly about can create a filter. Some examples are abortion, infidelity, eating habits (vegan, vegetarian, carnivore, gluten free), etc…
- Your political views can create filters based on your political leanings.
- Personal experiences with relationships of all kinds can create filters. If you have had difficulty in relationships, as opposed to having happiness and positive interactions, this will create a filter regarding how you interpret information in that arena. This includes childhood relationships with family, friends, teachers, etc.
- Even where you live creates filters based on local societal standards.

It's very important to understand your filters so you don't skew the information you convey to others. Without that understanding, you may disregard information that would be important to others. Information that may seem vague or unimportant to you may be very clear to someone else.

You need to be conscious of your filters and keep them as clear as you can in order to get the most accurate messages that you can.

Chapter 3
Mediumship

Practice

To make sure that my filters aren't getting in the way of interpreting information as accurately as possible I do a visualization that I call "putting my brain in a box".

I think of my brain as my ego, and then I picture what my ego would look like. To me, my ego looks like a large, beautiful amethyst crystal. It's sparkly and beautiful and likes to be noticed, even admired...hey, it's an ego! Once I got a visual on what my ego looks like, I imagined a beautifully carved wooden box filled with soft cushioning.

When I get prepared to do a reading, or work with energy in any other way, I visualize removing the crystal ego from myself and placing it gently in the box. I then close it, set it on a shelf, and get to work!

Ok, I Got Nothin'

What happens if you don't get any messages? Understand that it happens – to everyone! Sometimes those in spirit just don't want to talk, it's no reflection on you or your abilities. We knock on the door when we request communication, if they choose not to answer we must respect that it's their choice. Maybe they are busy doing something else, we don't necessarily know what they're up to. It seems like those who have crossed over would have more to do than wait around for us to ask them questions though. If whomever you are trying to reach doesn't answer, try again later. Or maybe try to contact someone else who may be available.

Another reason you don't get messages may be that you feel like you're under pressure, especially when you are just starting to offer readings to other people. You don't want to let them down. That's normal and it's okay. Take a few deep breaths to recenter yourself and start over. Be sure your energy field is pulled in to about 18-24 inches around you to ensure you aren't picking up on any ambient energies that may be in the room. Remember, too, that you can ask for help from your guides or the Divine Universe. Asking for help can connect you more securely to the spirit realm and that help is always at your disposal.

It could be that you are experiencing fear. Fear and excitement often feel the same physically, so if you are able to reframe your thinking to believe that you are experiencing excitement instead, you will have better results. Being excited about the possibility of helping someone through a difficult time may be all you need to serve them more completely and competently.

Here's a quick exercise to help you determine whether or not you are experiencing fear (or doubt or nervousness), and if you are how you can shift the feeling from fear to excitement.

Chapter 3

Mediumship

Exercise

Close your eyes for a moment and think about where in your body you feel fear or nervousness, not fear associated with physical danger, but rather the feeling you get when you experience fear due to circumstances involving feelings or thoughts. Do you get a lump in your throat? Maybe you feel a flutter in your heart area or feel a bit sick to your stomach. Perhaps you experience an all over feeling of dread. Whatever it is, make a mental note of it.

Now switch your thoughts to how your body feels when you are really emotionally excited about something. Are you feeling any of the physical sensations described above? If you are, it's an easy shift to convincing yourself you are excited about the opportunity to serve. If not then focus on the sensation that the excitement creates, your brain will be convinced that you are excited and behave accordingly.

If, after checking in with yourself, you still experience a blockage of energy flow, it may be because of the person you are reading. Even if someone asks for a reading, he or she may be nervous about it, especially if that person has never had a reading before. It can help to engage that person in light conversation to help put them more at ease. Avoid asking leading questions in doing so since you will want all of the information that you receive to come intuitively.

Sometimes people seek communication with loved ones through intuitive mediums/psychics, with little understanding of how intuition and psychic ability works. When this is the case, the person may try to block you from accessing some information while expecting you to access only the information that they are looking for. Very few people are skilled enough to compartmentalize to that extent, and they will invariably block you completely from reading them. As the reader in this instance, it's your responsibility to accurately assess the situation to figure out what's going on. You may need to explain that you have no control over the spirits who choose to come through, or over the information they choose to share. Some people will understand this and some won't, that is something over which you have no control.

Practice activities for Chapter 3

- *Continue to journal any experiences or dreams, paying special attention to subtle intuitions.*
- *Try contacting someone who has crossed over and journal the experience. If you are unable to contact the first person that you want to talk with, try someone else.*

Chapter Three Notes
_____
_____
_____

Chapter 3
Mediumship

Chapter 4: Managing and Manipulating Energy

Managing and manipulating energy, when done with intention, can produce amazing results. Before we get into what we can do with energy, beyond what we've already learned, let's discuss the difference between managing energy and manipulating energy.

Managing energy is working with your own energy, the energy inside of your personal space. Some examples of managing energy are meditating, changing thought processes (hopefully to more positive), and controlling your emotions. Physically you manage your energy anytime you eat, drink, sleep, or exercise...you get the idea. Anything that you do within your energy field is managing your energy.

Manipulating energy is when you use your energy to affect anything outside of your own energy field. Prayer is a good example of manipulating energy in that it is using your own energy (intention) to affect a situation outside of yourself. Energy healing is another example of how people use their own energy to affect something outside of themselves. Any transfer of energy from one person to another to facilitate some sort of healing or positive effect, is energy manipulation.

With practice, you can learn to both

Chapter 4
Managing and Manipulating Energy

manage your own energy and manipulate energy outside of yourself to heighten your own intuitive awareness, and to be of service. When you intentionally and effectively manage your own energy fields, you become more clear about other energies around you. The clarity you gain allows you to intuitively make better choices in your life, and to help others make better choices by presenting them with clear options.

Managing Your Energy

First, let's talk about ways to manage your own energy. Earlier I mentioned everyday activities we all do that are energy management. Let's get into greater detail on how to manage your energy more effectively. We covered some of this in Chapter One when you learned to control how large or small your energy field is by pulling it toward you or by pushing it out away from you. This is definitely a very effective tool. Any time that you take control of your own energy, you are empowering yourself to do whatever you want to do.

We're going to explore more ways in which you can manage your energy for everything from grounding to improving your health. A couple of basic tools you will use over and over again in managing your energy are visualization and intention. Using only these two tools, and following up your intentions with focused action, you can change anything in your life.

Intentional Breathing

Let's begin with the basics, breathing. Most of us are shallow breathers. We don't need to think about breathing in order to do it, so we don't. Because we aren't thinking about it, we tend not to breathe deeply, causing our bodies to not get enough oxygen. Without enough oxygen, we tend to be more stressed physically, which also affects us mentally and emotionally. By taking the time every day to focus on breathing deeply and slowly, we can all increase the oxygen in our blood and relax our bodies, which helps us be clearer and calmer. Deep breathing also helps to keep your lungs clear, preventing breathing problems in the future.

To get the greatest stress relieving benefit from your intentional breathing, try inhaling for a count of ten and then exhaling for a count of ten, breathing deeply into your abdomen so your belly expands. Repeat this four to five times and see how much more relaxed you feel, even in the midst of a busy day. If you remember to do this a few times throughout your day you will have better overall control of your own energy and your mood.

Do you need to increase your energy during that afternoon slump? Here's a breathing exercise to help you get more energy quickly. This is a great way to super-oxygenate the blood. Warning, don't do this exercise too late in the day or you may be awake longer than you'd like to be at night!

Chapter 4
Managing and Manipulating Energy

Deep Breathing Exercise

Inhale for a count of 5

Hold the breath for a count of 5

Exhale for a count of 5

Hold empty for a count of 5

Repeat 3 times

Along with breathing, you can add visualising to better manage not only your energy levels, but your physical body as well. The imagination is powerful. It literally creates the life that each person lives. What you imagine, you create. The more you imagine something, the more likely it is that you will create it in your life, whether positive or negative. This is probably more true with your physical health than it is in most other areas of your life. The way that you talk to yourself about how you feel is exactly how you are going to feel. You can create health or sickness, to a degree, just by thinking about it. For instance, if you are convinced that you're going to get a cold, you are more likely to get one. If, however, you believe yourself to be healthy and that you are going to stay that way, then you are far less likely to get a cold.

Beyond controlling, or influencing, minor things like getting or not getting a cold, you can use imagery to ease your own pain. Here is a simple exercise to help you identify and ease your own pain.

Pain Exercise

Close your eyes and take a deep breath. As you continue to breathe deeply and evenly, picture yourself standing in front of a full length mirror. Looking at your own image, picture it filling with a golden light. When the image of your body is filled with the golden light allow your eyes to "go out of focus" and let any "dark spots" appear wherever you may have pain, illness, or injury. Now visualize yourself reaching into the reflection and pulling out the dark spots, and noticing that the light fills the empty spaces that are created when you remove the dark spot.

Imagine that there is a cosmic recycling unit in the cosmos and toss the removed pieces into it, where they will be transformed into Light energy and returned to the Universe. Repeat this process until all of the dark spots have been removed. Sometimes the dark spots can represent mental or emotional blockages as well, and the visualisation will help just as much as if they represent physical pain. Now, check in with yourself. Are your painful spots gone? Is your energy increased? Make a mental note of these changes for future use. Remember that you can use any of the tools you are learning at any given time to help you to manage your own energy.

Another way to heal yourself using visualization is to picture clearly in your mind the sick or injured part of the body as fully healed and functioning properly. If you are unclear as to how the particular part of the

Chapter 4
Managing and Manipulating Energy

body should look when it's healthy you can look it up. Several websites have images of the human body where you can find how healthy body parts typically appear. Having this information will help you to be more clear in your intention. For instance, if you are working on balancing blood sugar levels, it helps to know what the pancreas looks like and where it is located. This visualization may or may not instantly heal the problem, but it will help to provide energy to exponentially promote the healing process.

Chakra Basics

Working directly within the chakra system is another great way to manage your own energy field. Very simply, the chakra system is a series of energy centers throughout your body. They are located at the base of the tailbone, just above the pubic bone, the solar plexus (near your navel), the heart, the throat, forehead, and the top of the head. Each Chakra correlates to a section of the body and has a color assigned to it. The following diagram shows the seven main chakras, their physical locations, and colors.

The chakra system is often used in energy healing modalities like Reiki, and a great deal of information is available online and in several excellent books. Extensive knowledge of the chakra system is not, however, necessary for you to understand how to use it for your own personal management purposes, so we will only cover the basics just to get you started.

This is a basic diagram of chakra locations along with their individual functions and colors.

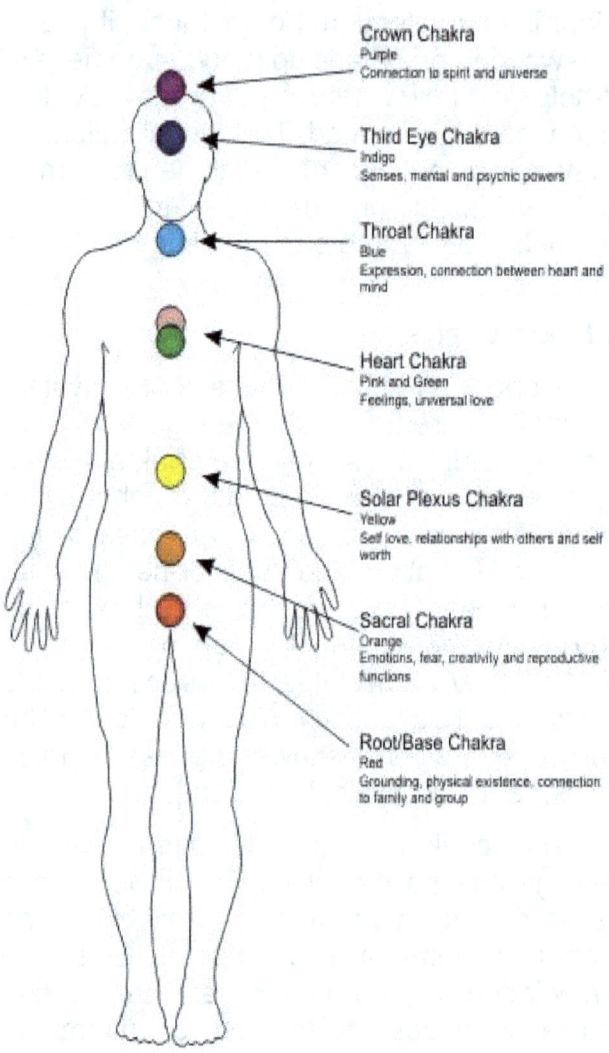

Chapter 4

Managing and Manipulating Energy

When working with the chakras, it is possible to manage each one individually or all seven main chakras at once. Chakras can get "blocked," meaning that energy flow through them is limited or stopped completely as we go about our daily lives. Any number of experiences can cause a chakra to be blocked. Emotional trauma, loss, illness, or even something as simple as driving in a stressful traffic situation can cause blockages in the chakras. Fortunately, in most cases, it is easy to unblock the chakras.

Chakra Exercise

For this exercise you can refer to the image on the previous page until you get used to how your chakras work. All of the chakras, except the throat, spin clockwise when they are open. The throat chakra, being the cross point between your head and body, spins counter-clockwise when it is open.

To find out if your chakras are open and working correctly, hold a pendulum in front of each chakra individually. If the pendulum swings in a clockwise circle for all but the throat chakra, then they are all open and functioning.

For most people, at least one chakra is not spinning or is spinning backwards. This is not a big deal! Using your hand, make a circular motion clockwise in front of the chakra for about 10 seconds, then check it again. The direction of the energy should have corrected. If the direction of the energy spinning the pendulum has not corrected, spin the energy with your hand again. Note that the throat Chakra is the only Chakra spinning counter clockwise when it is functioning properly. This is because the throat chakra is the cross point between the head and the body. The right side of the brain controls the left side of the body and vice versa.

If, after spinning the energy of the chakra a second time, the direction is not corrected, you may want to take time to meditate in order to gain clarity on why the blockage is there. Which chakra is blocked should indicate to you what the energetic or emotional issue is that you need to release in order to return to a healthy energy flow. If the blockage is particularly stubborn, or caused by a major trauma, it may be in your best interest to seek the help of an Intuitive professional or counselor.

Processing through the feelings that cause blockages is paramount to opening yourself to clear intuitive information. Issues left unaddressed create judgement and judgement creates filters. Those filters, as discussed in Chapter Three, prevent readers from clearly perceiving and conveying information.

That being said, there are times when it's to your benefit to intentionally close or cover your chakras. Depending on the situation, you may choose to "protect" one or all of your chakras. Some circumstances when you may want to do this include, but are not limited to, being in a large crowd of people. This may especially apply if the crowd is not of like

Chapter 4
Managing and Manipulating Energy

mind or is chaotic. Walking through a busy store, mall, or airport can be overwhelming for energy sensitive people whose chakras are wide open. Another circumstance is when you are with people with whom you don't feel emotionally safe. (Family holidays, anyone?) The workplace is another place where many people may need to keep their energy centers protected because they aren't able to express who they are spiritually without facing ridicule.

Chakra Energy Flow Control Exercise

To intentionally control the amount of energy flowing through the chakras, you can visualize that each chakra has a camera shutter attached to the front of it. Using your imagination and intention, close each shutter as much as you are comfortable with closing it. You can use this imagery technique on one or as many of your chakras as you feel necessary based on the situation. For instance, if you have a lot of work to get done and are being distracted by intuitive feelings or psychic messages, you may want to cover your third eye and limit the flow of energy coming into your crown. Using the image of a camera shutter allows you to choose how much energy flows into, and out of, a chakra by deciding to what percentage you want to cover a particular chakra. In this case you may choose to completely cover the third eye and cover the crown to 90%, vice versa, or any configuration you prefer.

This example is just to demonstrate for you how to cover chakras temporarily. When you are home, or in some other comfortable place and the energy around you has changed, remember to uncover your chakras. Once you have taken control of your energy in any intentional way, you become responsible for making sure that you manage your energy. It's important to remember also that if you leave any chakras covered for too long you risk creating a blockage that wasn't previously there.

Vibrational Healing

Now that we've learned a little bit about chakras, let's focus on more ways to work with those energy centers to enhance and balance the energy flow from those centers. All of the tools you've used so far have been internal, imagination, and visualization. Now we are going to make some noise! That's right, we are adding sound vibration to the intention. There are several ways to use sound waves to shake up energy, three of which we will discuss here.

Toning

The first technique is *Toning*. Toning is using sound waves created by vocal chords to move energy through the chakras. This technique has been employed for a long time in many cultures (think Gregorian Chants) to balance the energy of the body. It can also be

Chapter 4
Managing and Manipulating Energy

used in self-healing for problematic throat and sinus issues. The vibration created by toning can break loose phlegm and allow for easier breathing.

Overall, toning raises your body's vibrational level creating more energy for you! Try this quick exercise using toning.

Toning Exercise

*Stand comfortably with your knees slightly bent (not locked) and take a deep yet comfortable breath. Visualize your chakras. Open your mouth a bit and begin to make a sound that comes from your throat. That sound is **toning**! Now place one or both hands in front of your root chakra as you begin to tone again. While toning slowly glide your hands upward toward your head. When your hands reach your mouth move them in a quick motion like you are throwing something into the air. This is the point where you let your voice fade until you are finished toning - another two to three seconds should be sufficient. It may help to envision each chakra lighting up in its own color as you move your hands upward, indicating they are energized.*

Now pay attention to how you feel. Do you feel lighter or more balanced and peaceful? You can do this as many times as needed to achieve the result you want.

The primary advantage to using toning is you don't need any special equipment or tools, just your own voice. You can also help other people to tone using this technique. When your voice joins another voice, the energy is more powerful, so when helping another tone, have that person tone with you.

If you are driving a distance and getting road weary, you can easily do toning right there in the driver's seat. Using only your voice and visualization, you can move energy through all of your chakras and help yourself become more focused again! To sum it up, toning is easy to do and can be used anywhere, as long as making the sound isn't an issue.

Tibetan Singing Bowls

Another tool that a lot of people like to use are Tibetan singing bowls. The bowls come in various sizes and tones. They are usually made of copper, although some are made of crystal. Singing bowls make a sound when you move a wooden mallet around the outside edge of the bowl in a smooth motion. Each bowl has its own particular sound based on the size of the bowl and the thickness of the metal. The larger the bowl, the deeper the resonant sound will be. Crystal singing bowls are often made intentionally to resonate with particular chakras.

Chapter 4
Managing and Manipulating Energy

Singing bowls are often used during meditations or energy healing sessions since the sounds they make are generally soothing and aid the users in reaching higher levels of consciousness. The vibrational tone created when tapping the side of the bowl with the mallet can help to clear the mind, promoting greater clarity and concentration during meditation. Some psychics and energy healers use singing bowls before meeting with clients to clear the space for the work to be done, and again after to clear any negative or heavy energy left behind by the session.

Tibetan Singing Bowl Exercise

To clear chakras and auras, simply tap the side of the bowl with the mallet and gently holding the bowl move it up and down slowly in front of you. You may need to tap the bowl a few times to ensure that it is still vibrating and "singing." Do this until you feel refreshed and relaxed. If you like, you can check your chakras with your pendulum to make sure they are open.

Drums

If you prefer a more rhythmic sound, drums may be a good choice for you in clearing your personal energy or surroundings. Hand-held open backed drums (Native 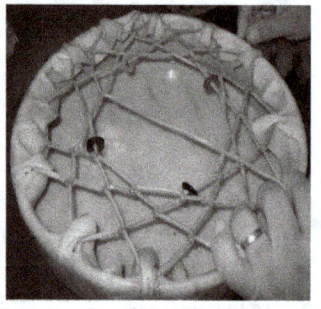 American or Celtic style) are particularly good for energy cleansing. Like the singing bowls, the larger the drum the deeper the sound and the more vibration they generate. Shamans around the world use drums in Shamanic Healings.

In traditional Native American culture, the drum is considered a sacred instrument and is often referred to as a "Grandmother" or "Grandfather." It is used as a tool for prayer and meditation, and drumming is usually accompanied by songs sung in the native language.

Chapter 4
Managing and Manipulating Energy

If you want to use your drum for meditation, and don't know any Native American songs, play the drum softly with the rhythm of a gentle heart beat. This is an easy, relaxing rhythm that helps you focus and keeps your mind from wandering.

You can use a drum to quickly clear your aura or someone else's aura. This exercise works best with two people taking turns drumming for each other.

Drumming Exercise

Have your partner stand comfortably. Stand to the side of your partner facing her shoulder. Hold the drum in front of your partner at about knee level, with the back of the drum toward your partner. Hit the drum once at knee level, then at hip/pelvis level, then at the heart level, and finally at face level. Immediately after you hit the drum at face level, lift the drum up and over to the back of their head. The drum should still be vibrating as you lift it over their head. They may feel a little off balance, so be sure to stay right there with them until the vibrations settle in, this usually only takes about a minute.

When your partner is ready, switch places. Have them follow the same instructions as they clear your energy with the drum. It's that quick and easy!

With so many ways to manage your energy, something is sure to resonate!

Manipulating Energy

At the point when you go from clearing your own energy to clearing a space (or a room), you go from managing energy to manipulating energy. Remember in Chapter One when you were instructed how to set a space in a room? That, too, is manipulating energy. So far in this chapter, we've talked about ways to use energy for healing the self and others. Now we're going to discuss different ways to use energy to affect the world around us for the better.

Energy can be manipulated to make life easier, less stressful and more fun! This, my friends, is where the magic is! Moving energy with intention IS magical, and practical. In Chapter Two we talked about how everything is made of energy and how that relates to communicating with those who have crossed over. Now we're going to take our understanding that everything is made of energy into the physical world and start to play with it!

Let's begin with something none of us enjoy, traffic. How much time have we all wasted sitting in traffic that goes nowhere? Did you know that you can influence traffic flow? You can! Traffic is energy just like everything else, and it's energy in motion, which makes it even easier to affect. The real trick is to have the intention of traffic flowing for the *highest good of everyone*! After all, if no one else can move, neither can you. Here is an easy trick to get you all moving…

Chapter 4
Managing and Manipulating Energy

Traffic Exercise

Say, out loud or to yourself, "Thank you for getting everyone where they are going easily, smoothly, safely, and quickly for the highest good of all." Continue to repeat it while also mentally sending energy through the windshield to the traffic in front of you. You can make this easier by steering with the heel of your hands and facing your palms through the windshield. Visualize the traffic ahead of you, even miles ahead of you, speeding up. Visualize traffic flow free of construction backups and free of accidents. Repeat this exercise until all traffic is flowing well.

There may be times when you have to start the process again because traffic slows down or stops again, that's ok, just keep doing it. Also, if the exact wording "Thank you for getting everyone where they are going easily, smoothly, safely and quickly for the highest good of all" isn't comfortable for you, paraphrase with your own words as long the intent is the same. This will work most of the time. Remember, though, not everything is in your control and delays may be for your safety and best interest, even if you don't know it. Keep practicing. The more you practice, the better you will get at moving traffic.

Sometimes we find ourselves in uncomfortable positions in life, not because of what we did but because of what others have done. Whether at work, at home, or out in public, we sometimes feel the intensity of other people's anger or hostility. It doesn't feel good regardless of why it's happening.

You can do something about it, however. You can visualize sending those people so much LOVE that they calm down and hopefully reevaluate their behavior. It can work in simple circumstances, like getting your kids to settle down, or in more intense situations like a potentially violent exchange between strangers in public. Here is a quick and easy visualization to help you diffuse difficult situations.

Pink Ribbons Of Light Exercise

Using your imagination, envision you are holding onto a short stick that is attached to a pink ribbon made of light. Think of the ribbons used in rhythmic gymnastics. The ribbon can be as long as you need it to be. Now use visualization to swirl the ribbons around whomever or whatever is upsetting you. **Continue swirling the ribbons until you feel better!** *Some situations will take longer for the projected Love to have an effect, be patient and keep working at it. For sending healing energy to someone it may help to visualize the ribbons as emerald green. This is a simple yet very effective tool for transforming energy.*

Chapter 4
Managing and Manipulating Energy

Loving thoughts alone can transform a difficult situation, however when you add a visualization and action, the transformation can happen much more quickly. You can also use this technique to swirl pink ribbons of light around yourself when you are upset. Although this technique can help you feel better, especially when you use it on yourself, it isn't a replacement for emotional and mental self care. You still have to pay attention to your energy and the energies that surround you in order to be in the best place you can be within yourself.

You can also use energy manipulation to clear energy from a home or business and set a new energy in its place. This is similar to what we did in the beginning of this course, but much more involved. We will explore this in greater detail in Chapter Five.

When people get really good at energy manipulation, they can do the things we read about like telekinesis, levitation, cloudbusting, moving weather fronts, and the like. With desire and practice, any one of us can make these things happen. Anything is possible!

Ethical Guidelines For Energy Manipulation

Just because anything is possible doesn't give us carte blanche to do whatever we want to do. There are still guidelines to follow and Universal Laws* to abide by. Like energy attracts like energy. Whatever we put out energetically will return to us.

Keeping this in mind, here are some simple guidelines to follow when working with energy and intuition.

- Use energy and your intuition only for the highest outcome for all involved.
- Use it only to help, never to harm.
- Using energy to manipulate the behaviour of others should only be used to prevent them from harming themselves or another person, including you.
- Energy manipulation must always be done with the highest respect for all, whether in or out of a body.

By always keeping the intention for the highest order of love and light, we are able to enjoy our lives as we develop intuitive abilities. Knowing that there is more to learn, and there always will be.

Practice activities for Chapter Four

- *Practice controlled breathing, imagery and visualization and journal your results.*
- *Practice using energy to control traffic and to employ "pink ribbons" when needed.*

Chapter 4
Managing and Manipulating Energy

Chapter Four Notes

Chapter 5: Paranormal Investigation

As you advance in training and experience, you may be drawn to *Paranormal Investigation* and/or *Spirit Releasing.* Paranormal Investigation is the study of paranormal energy. Spirit Releasing is working with energy to help release spirits who are "stuck" on the Earth plane. It's time to learn how to identify energy fluctuations and to communicate with spirits outside of doing psychic readings.

If you are reading this book as part of a class, your teacher will set up a safe place for your first "paranormal investigation." If you are reading this book on your own, this chapter will guide you in your first "paranormal investigation." Either way, since this book and course are intuition based, the focus should be on intuition and discerning energy fluctuations as opposed to finding physical evidence. But, since it's so much fun to film orbs, listen to Electronic Voice Phenomenon, or EVPs, and try to catch an apparition in a still shot, I've included information on how to do those things correctly in this chapter.

When you start your paranormal investigation, keep your focus on reading energy using intuition, and move slowly through your chosen location, paying

Chapter 5
Paranormal Investigation

attention to how each room feels if you are indoors. If your location is outdoors, pay attention to any energy fluctuations as you move from one area to another. Again, move slowly enough to notice the differences. Stop to have brief discussions with your companion(s). They may have noticed things that you didn't notice or you may be able to confirm with each other what you are experiencing.

Be mindful of any ghosts or spirits who may try to communicate with you. Ask questions to see if you can get responses. This is a chance to experience actual conversations with those outside of the physical world. DO NOT PROVOKE!!

Safety First!

Physical Safety

- Ideally, you won't go on private property to investigate if you have not been invited or received permission. This may be obvious, but if you go on private property without permission, you could be arrested or even shot at. For this reason, you may want to be careful visiting cemeteries without permission unless you know for certain that it is public land. Church owned cemeteries are still private property.
- If you are a casual researcher, which most are, and are doing paranormal research out of curiosity, or even just for fun, you may be better off sticking to public areas.

Be aware though that even in public areas, there are rules to follow to avoid arrest or other run-ins with law enforcement. Parks and cemeteries often have posted hours, many of which prohibit people from being there after dark. Some towns have curfews that apply to everyone, although some apply just to minors. Most municipalities have noise ordinances after certain times, usually around 10 PM. So if you are with people who spook easily, and are likely to scream often and/or loudly, you may want to keep that in mind.

- Regardless of whether you are on private property or public property, there are other common sense safety precautions to take.
- Tripping hazards exist both inside and outside, so bring a flashlight and wear tennis shoes or hiking boots.
- Even though it will probably be dark when you are investigating, don't wear reflective clothing or shoes because reflections can give you false readings on visual electronic equipment.
- Bring your cell phone, but keep it set on silent. Noise, especially if a phone vibrates can cause false readings on audio equipment. Smartphones are so advanced now that you can download apps onto them that record EVPs, take night vision video and have excellent digital cameras. Unless you have a need for extremely sensitive electronic equipment, your iPhone or Android

should work well for capturing evidence. Make sure that your phone is fully charged as batteries tend to die quickly in high energy situations.
- Always have at least one other person with you. When roaming around in the dark your have a higher risk of injury and there should always be someone to help. There is safety in numbers. Plus you may need someone for verification reasons later. Also, I would never take anyone under the age of 18 with me unless it was my own child or the child's legal guardian is also going on the investigation.

Energetic Safety

- As with any situation in which you are working spiritual energy, always have the intention for the highest order of love and light.
- Project loving and respectful energy by thinking loving and respectful thoughts. What you emanate is what you will get back, so make sure everyone in your group is on the same page energetically.
- The group energy is very important because if even one member of the group is there to scare themselves for thrill seeking reasons, or with the idea that they are going to wield banishing powers, it will affect the entire group and possibly the outcome of the investigation.
- Use the golden rule and treat everyone, both with and without bodies, with respect.

For your first few paranormal investigations, you will probably want to go with someone who has experience. If this person is not your *Intuitive You!* instructor, you may want to look for a local paranormal investigation group. You can do an internet search to find paranormal investigation teams in your area. Each group has its own energy, its own "feel" about it. Check with your own intuition to see if it feels like a good fit for you. If one doesn't feel right, move on to the next one until you find a group with which you are comfortable.

Before entering the place where the investigation is to take place, stop to set your intention for yourself and anyone who is with you. A lot of people refer to this step as placing protection around everyone. Whatever you choose to call it, be sure to do it! Following are some ways to set your intention. Feel free to use one or all of them based on what you feel the need is at the time.

- Surround yourself and your group with white light. This seems to be the most common practice used by paranormal investigation groups, especially those who use psychics in their investigations.
- Set an intention/say a prayer for only positive communication with any spirits you may encounter during the course of the investigation.
- Ask permission to enter "their home" and state you're coming in with only the

Chapter 5
Paranormal Investigation

highest respect for them. If you feel like the request is answered with "No," you will probably want to leave and find somewhere else to investigate.

When you have completed the investigation, stop outside of the location again to thank the Spirits for letting you spend time there and for any communication that may have taken place. Also, ask that all of the spirits stay there rather than following you or anyone in the group home. Have everyone check their own energy to be certain that the living, breathing humans didn't leave any part of their spirits there, as well.

Example

During a paranormal investigation we visited a mansion that I use a lot for Intuitive You! field trips. In the basement of this location is a theater where a local theater group performs plays. The theater is usually active with paranormal energy, and this evening was no exception. There were props set up on the stage for a performance taking place the following evening. We must have arrived right after a rehearsal because we could feel the excitement in the air even though all of the actors had already left.

One of my students mentioned that as a child she used put on singing and dancing performances for her family. I thought that was cute, but didn't think much else about it as we continued the tour up through the next three levels of the building. The class was doing a great job identifying spirits and energy fluctuations, and everyone was having a great time. We finished the tour, thanked our hosts and when outside where we had a closing ceremony. During the closing ceremony I thanked the spirits of the mansion for communicating with us and asked that they stay there. Everything was great, we all went home.

The following week when the class met again to begin Intuitive You! The Next Level, that student seemed like she was half asleep. When we started talking about the field trip she shared that she had felt just "out of it" all week. At that point it occurred to me that I had not scanned everyone to make sure they hadn't left part of their own spirits at the mansion. I immediately bi-located to the mansion, and sure enough there she was. Her inner child was happily singing and dancing on the stage!

It took some convincing, but I got her to come with me back to her current body. (I know this might sound strange to people who are new to paranormal investigations, but it happens more than you might think.) Once that part of the soul was returned, she felt like herself again.

This was a big lesson for me to make sure that I check every member of my team every single time I take them on an investigation.

Chapter 5
Paranormal Investigation

Paranormal Investigation Etiquette

As paranormal researchers, we carry a great deal of responsibility; for the safety of ourselves and our team members, for the property upon which we are investigating, and for those souls we are investigating. We must be respectful to the property owners, public or private, and take responsibility for any physical damages that may be caused during the investigation. Accidents can happen, and each team member has to be mature enough to take responsibility for any damage they might cause.

Regarding the souls we are investigating, we are there to make contact, to attempt to understand, and to experience whatever we may encounter. Understanding that many of us who are drawn to the paranormal are sensitive souls ourselves, we have to have respect for the fact that they may still be here because they want to be. Some are stuck and looking for help, and if we have the ability we may certainly help them to move on. However, it is NOT our job to come in and banish anybody. We have only a limited perception when it comes to the greater Universe/Multiverse, and usually won't have enough information to determine whether or not banishment (or sending them "to the light") is even a good idea.

The paranormal is simply something outside of our normal physical perception. We may have no way of knowing whether what or who we are seeing, hearing or sensing is someone who has crossed over from our plane of existence into pure energy (spirit) or someone who is simply alive and well in another plane of existence. Either way, to us it is paranormal. And, either way, we can learn from them.

The Toys and How to Use Them

For the most part, cellular phones are so advanced now that your phone alone can be used for a number "ghost hunting" devices. First, the cameras on the new phones are high quality and can capture energy unseen by the human eye with great accuracy.

Here is an example of a photo taken with a cell phone during a ghost walk in Wisconsin. The man who took the photo simply asked nicely for any spirits who are present to show themselves. No one on the walk saw her with our naked eyes. If you look closely you can see that she has no discernable facial features.

Chapter 5
Paranormal Investigation

There are several apps in the Google Play Store and the App Store that have voice recorders which are more sensitive than the regular recorder already in your phone for recording electronic voice phenomena (EVP). In choosing the best EVP recording app or device, be sure to do research before you choose to purchase one separate from your phone. Read reviews and check the frequency range the device covers. You ideally want a recorder that picks up the widest possible range of frequencies.

Another piece of equipment used by paranormal investigators is called a Spirit Box. The Spirit Box scans am and fm radio waves to pick up sounds that the human ear misses. You can purchase these devices at several online retailers.

And lastly, the electromagnetic field, or EMF, detector. This device measures changes in electrical fields. Be careful with your interpretations of the information you see because the needle will spike near elevated electrical grids as well as ghosts.

The Role of Psychics in Paranormal Investigations

Because of our limited understanding of all possible scenarios, and because electronic equipment is also not able to distinguish one *type* of energy from another, it is helpful to have psychics on hand who are able to communicate clearly with the energies that are present.

A good psychic who has a clear understanding of energy, how it works, and also of his or her own filters, is the best kind to have on a paranormal investigation team. A well grounded psychic who is versed in several forms of paranormal communication, including mediumship, intuition, interstellar and interdimensional communication, will serve your investigation and teach you well. It is important to be joy-based rather than fear-based. As a joy-based psychic, you will be more open to exploring all possibilities than if you are fear-based.

Psychics can understand the differences and fluctuations of energy in a way that equipment simply can't. Having psychics on an investigation can help the team to make sense of the information that they collect.

Confirming or Debunking Paranormal Research and Information

Let's face it, the field of paranormal research has had its share of frauds over the years. People have doctored photos for as long as photography has existed. People have probably lied for longer than we've even had speech! When you add in that most people are suspicious by nature, it's no wonder that so many paranormal researchers are resistant to sharing their findings, or to absolutely confirm findings. Those who do publicly confirm their findings, if they are smart, go to great lengths to debunk their own work before someone else has a chance to do so. Keeping this in mind,

Chapter 5
Paranormal Investigation

remember that some people will never be convinced no matter how real or authentic evidence is. Fortunately, those particular people are usually not serious paranormal researchers, so their opinion doesn't matter anyway.

So, how do we go about confirming or debunking our own evidence? We can do this using equipment, either visual or auditory.

Visual Orbs

These can appear in pictures for a number of reasons and in a number of ways. Some are actual representations of energy, and most are not. To determine whether or not an orb is authentic, it's helpful to magnify it in order to see it more clearly.

- Most often what appears as an orb is usually dust reflecting light in the camera lens. It can also be droplets of water, even when it isn't raining.
- Humidity can cause the same effect.
- The third most common cause of false orbs in photos is reflected light, even from a dim or seemingly distant source.
- Also, if each picture has an orb in the same placement, or all of the orbs are identical, you probably just have a spot on your lens. If these four causes can be ruled out then it's time to investigate further.

When orbs are actually legitimate, they generally have a glow to them that dust or water doesn't. Be careful, however, because some light sources can create that effect, as well. Authentic orbs may have "faces" in them. They may not be perfectly round or they may appear to be moving, even in the still shots. Orbs can also appear as different sizes. You may notice that some people tend to have orbs near them in pictures. When the same person has orbs near them in several photos taken over a period of time, you are likely catching orbs in the photos.

Ghostly Figures Or Apparitions

This is a pretty rare phenomenon, but it can happen. The actual image of an energy being is captured in a photo, like earlier in this chapter. If you do catch an image in a photo, look for ways to debunk it before declaring it a ghost. Look for nearby reflective surfaces that could distort a picture, whether the image was taken inside or outside. The curves on cars can create some pretty interesting illusions that can look like apparitions. As with orbs, light sources can also create the illusion of figures in pictures so double check where any light could be coming from. The same goes for columns of light.

Be especially aware of your surroundings when taking pictures of buildings from the outside. Nearly anything can reflect on windows, causing images that may or may not actually be there. This is even more likely if the building has older windows with uneven glass.

Chapter 5
Paranormal Investigation

Example

During an investigation at the site of a mass murder, one of our team members took a picture of the outside of the house where many of the murders took place, along with several other pictures around the property. Later, when he was going through the pictures, he noticed something in the top floor window that he didn't recall seeing when he took the photo. It appeared to be a green and red toy monkey. A couple of people from the team went into the upstairs bedroom to see if an object fitting that description was indeed in the window. Not only was there nothing like that in window, there were no toys in the room.

The photographer had a feeling there was a reasonable explanation for the anomaly, so he kept looking for anything that would explain the monkey in the window. After about an hour he figured it out. Down the street was a neighbor's house that had a green and red hummingbird feeder hanging in a tree in their front yard. The house was easily at least a city block or more away from where we were investigating, and had he not seen the feeder he could have claimed the photo as paranormal evidence. Trusting his intuition and having integrity led him to debunk his finding before anyone else could.

Audio

Here's where a lot of false readings can occur, primarily because EVP (Electronic Voice Phenomena) are notoriously difficult to hear. And, when you do hear an EVP, it's even harder to understand. As mentioned above, the equipment used to capture EVP is getting more sensitive, which may lead to more clear auditory recordings.

One way to guarantee false readings is to whisper in the room where the audio recording equipment is set up. Even the most subtle whisper can be picked up by sensitive equipment. To allow for a margin of error, most ghost hunting groups will choose a one syllable word that everyone uses to identify when they've made a noise. This way when they listen to the recordings later there is no confusion.

To avoid the need for later confirmation, no one should ever be alone during a paranormal investigation. By using the buddy system, you ensure that if an event does happen there are at least two people who can verify it.

Spirit Rescue and Release

Sometimes during a paranormal investigation a spirit appears who is in need of help. Armed with knowledge and experience, a psychic investigator will be able to help the spirit move on and find peace. To become proficient in discerning

Chapter 5
Paranormal Investigation

which spirits need help and which are happy where they are, let's talk about some different types of hauntings.

Residual Haunting

The most common type of haunting, a residual haunting occurs when a ghost repeats the same action over and over. The ghost is stuck in a repetitive occurrence. Sometimes the ghost continues to experience its death, especially if the death was unexpected or difficult, and the ghost is still trying to process the experience. Sometimes a residual haunting occurs if the ghost goes to work every day. Regardless of the reason, the ghost repeats the same actions, often at the same time every day. The ghosts in residual hauntings aso don't interact with people who try to interact with them.

Intelligent Haunting

These are the ghosts who will attempt to speak to you. They will try to get your attention however they can. They may be choosing to stay here, or they may be wanting help to leave. Either way, they want to talk and their message to be heard.

Poltergeist Haunting

Poltergeist translated from German literally means "noisy ghost." They can be tricksters or malicious, although by most accounts they are usually not malicious. They sometimes move objects and generally just play around with people. (In my house I have one that rattles dishes that need to be washed.) Sometimes a poltergeist will be around causing havoc for a long time, and sometimes it only happens once or a few times. There doesn't seem to be any consistency to this type of haunting.

Animal Spirit Haunting

Spirits of pets and other animals can also stay around after death. Without explanation as to why they stay around, we assume that they simply don't want to leave their families. Many people have reported seeing dogs or cats, some have even tripped over spirit cats winding around their legs, like cats do.

These are the types of spirits you're most likely to come into contact with while doing a paranormal investigation. Again, DO NOT PROVOKE! Provoking a ghost to elicit a response is likely to make the ghost angry and there is no need to do this. If ghosts are present who want to communicate, they will. If they don't want to communicate, they won't. It's just like when you're doing a mediumship reading, you can invite communication and it's up to them to answer.

At times you may find spirits who seem disoriented or lost. They may be looking for someone who can help them. If they know you can communicate with them, then you

Chapter 5
Paranormal Investigation

are probably the person they are looking for. In this case, your best course of action is to call for help from a *being of light*, an angel or whomever the spirit tells you may be able to help. It is paramount that you understand that your role here is to ask for help from the other side. If you are with another person who is more experienced than you are, it's a good idea to ask them to help by adding their intention that the spirit find peace or "go to the light."

As with any skill, some people have a knack for helping ghosts or spirits release to go to the light and some don't. If that type of experience doesn't happen for you, it's okay. It just means that your talents lie elsewhere. Intuition is a very individual thing, it works differently for different people. The only way to find out how it works for you is to try different things.

Practice activities for Chapter Five

- *Practice feeling the energy around you and make a note of when and how it changes.*
- *Familiarize yourself with safety suggestions and etiquette guidelines for paranormal investigations.*

Chapter Five Notes

Chapter 6: The Paranormal Investigation Field Trip

Now you're ready to get out there, have fun and explore with your newly discovered or enhanced skills! The field trip is where you get the chance to do just that as you embark on a paranormal exploration to somewhere known to have paranormal activity and is also a safe location both physically and metaphysically. If you are reading this book and studying independently, you will want to do some research in your local area. Many businesses that have had paranormal activity reported to them allow people to come in during regular business hours to see if they can pick up any paranormal energy. Some charge a fee or request that you make a purchase, especially if the business is a restaurant. Some have scheduled tours that provide a great opportunity for you to practice.

For those who are reading this book as part of the *Intuitive You!* course, your instructor will have chosen a place for your field trip. You can trust that the teacher knows how to find the best possible location for the field trip.

Field Trip Checklist

There are a few things that you will want to bring with you when you go on your field trip.

Here's a quick checklist of suggested items. Use your discretion based on where you are going.

- Wear comfortable, non reflective clothing and shoes
- Flashlight
- Charged cell phone
- Notebook and pen
- Another person who is both interested and trustworthy
- An open, yet discriminating mind

Before you enter the field trip location, remember to place an intention of safety around you and your group as described in Chapter Five. Pay attention to how you feel, physically and emotionally, before you enter the location. While you're there, also pay attention to how you feel and how your feelings change as you move through the location. Then check your feelings again after leaving the location. If you feel unusually tired, nauseous, unable to concentrate, or just a little "off" then you probably left part of yourself there. Most often, if a part of you stays behind it's because you found some part of the experience to be very interesting or enjoyable. To retrieve that part of you,

Chapter 6

A Paranormal Investigation Field Trip

simply close your eyes and mentally follow where you've been until you sense that part of you still there. To bring yourself back, just call yourself back to your body. It really is that easy!

Happy Exploring!

Paranormal Investigation Follow Up

After some time has gone by (it could be a few hours or a few days) following your investigation, take some time to reflect on the experience. If you are taking the class with an *Intuitive You!* teacher, your teacher will set time aside for a discussion. If you are using this book as an independent student, make time to meditate on your experience or find someone who is experienced in paranormal investigation and discuss your experience with them.

Think back to how you felt before, during and immediately after the investigation. Have you gained any insights that were not immediately apparent to you? Have any particular thoughts, feelings or events that happened during the investigation stuck with you? As you reflect back to the experience simply allow any images or sounds that you may have forgotten drift into your awareness.

Were you able to experience energy changes as you moved through the location? You may want to journal what that experience was like for you. Think about what you learned regarding your ability to sense energy changes and how you can use that ability to make your life easier in general. Since everything is energy, having an awareness of how you experience energy can help you to manage your own energetic field more proficiently in your day to day life. Whether or not you choose to ever do another paranormal investigation, you have gained a valuable skill!

Chapter Six Notes

_____

_____

_____

_____

_____

_____

_____

_____

_____

_____

_____

Chapter 6
A Paranormal Investigation Field Trip

A Note from the Author

First, thank you for allowing me to be a part of your spiritual journey! This is the first of three books in this series, with each book progressing in both technical intuitive skill and personal growth.

Our spiritual journeys on this planet are so individual and intuition is only part of the story. Personal emotional and mental health and growth is the most important part of learning to trust our intuitive/psychic abilities. Along the path of our spiritual journeys we will all come across our own lessons, more often than we prefer those lessons are personal. Many of those lessons involve relationships of all types, and our behaviors within the context of how we cope with ourselves in regards to other people.

We understand that we are spiritual beings, therefore any spiritual growth necessarily has to include personal growth as well. Remain open to growing all of you and watch the magic unfold!

A Note from the Author

Author Contact Information

    In addition to creating and teaching Intuitive You!, Kristina is also a Spiritual Advisor and Coach, retreat facilitator and speaker. Kristina facilitates a variety of workshops and retreats to help you in your Spiritual and Personal Growth. From Intuitive You! To The Twelve Universal Laws for Manifesting, her workshops and retreats are the perfect way to help you reach enlightenment!

    For more information and to register for upcoming events visit her website at http://kristinabloom.com. You can contact her at Kristina@kristinabloom.com.

Rev. Kristina L. Bloom
Psychic and Spiritual Advisor
kristina@kristiniabloom.com
http://kristinabloom.com

https://www.facebook.com/pages/Kristina-L-Bloom-Spiritual-Advisor/449431815166991

Index

angel
  angels, 45, 46, 56, 131
apparition, 112
Apparitions
  apparition, 125
awareness
  aware, 32, 50, 54, 55, 64, 88, 136, 137

banish, 120
being watched, 15, 62
Breathing, 89, 90

Centering, 40
chakra, 92, 93, 95, 96, 97, 99
clairalience, 5, 18
Clairaudience, 10
clairgustance, 5
Clairsentience, 15
clairvoyance, 5, 7
clarity, 15, 41, 65, 68, 69, 88, 96, 101
Clearing, 31, 33
communication, 4, 5, 7, 15, 18, 21, 24, 34, 44, 54, 56, 73, 77, 82, 84, 117, 123, 131
corporeal, 10, 59, 66

deja vu, 21
discernment, 24, 51
Divination, 42
Divination Tools
  divination, 42
Divine, 28, 42, 82
Divining, 45
Divining rods, 45

electromagnetic, 122
Electronic Voice Phenomena, 128
empathy, 15, 68
energetic, 1, 34, 37, 59, 96, 137
energy, 3, 7, 15, 27, 28, 29, 30, 31, 32, 33, 37, 38, 39, 40, 41, 43, 44, 45, 46, 50, 52, 54, 55, 59, 60, 61, 62, 63, 64, 65, 66, 67, 75, 79, 81, 82, 84, 87, 88, 89, 90, 91, 92, 93, 94, 95, 96, 97, 98, 99, 100, 101, 102, 104, 105, 106, 107, 108, 109, 110, 112, 113, 115, 116, 117, 118, 121, 123, 124, 126, 131, 134, 136
energy field, 38, 39, 40, 45, 50, 82, 87, 88, 92
energy management, 88
Energy Manipulation, 109
ethically, 50
Etiquette, 120
EVP, 122, 128

filters
  filter, 41, 42, 62, 64, 80, 81, 96, 123

ghost, 121, 126, 128, 129, 130
ghosts, 113
Ghostly Figures, 125
goosebumps, 15, 62
Grounding, 40

haunting
  hauntings, 73, 129, 130
heal

healing, 92
highest good, 41, 105, 106

intention, 32, 37, 41, 42, 43, 73, 87, 89, 92, 97, 98, 105, 109, 115, 116, 117, 131, 135
intuition, 1, 2, 3, 4, 10, 15, 21, 24, 28, 30, 31, 41, 42, 46, 51, 54, 55, 64, 67, 70, 72, 74, 77, 84, 109, 112, 113, 116, 123, 127, 140
intuitive, 1, 2, 4, 7, 18, 24, 28, 30, 49, 54, 55, 56, 62, 63, 64, 67, 69, 72, 84, 88, 96, 97, 109, 140

journey, 42, 51, 140
judgment, 2, 38, 59, 65, 66

mediumship
  medium, 4, 18, 78, 123, 131
message
  messages, 10, 42, 52, 70, 78, 79, 80, 129
metaphysical, 4, 5, 7, 31, 43, 45
Multiverse, 120

oracle, 45, 50
Oracle cards, 50
orbs, 112, 125, 126

paranormal, 1, 5, 24, 55, 112, 113, 114, 116, 117, 118, 119, 120, 122, 123, 124, 127, 128, 130, 132, 134, 136, 137
paranormal investigation, 112, 113, 116, 117, 118, 123, 128, 130, 136, 137

pendulum, 39, 43, 44, 45, 95, 102
Personal Energy Awareness, 38
power, vi, 29, 31, 39, 64, 77
Prayer, 87
project, 27
projected, 7, 107
psychic, vi, vii, 1, 2, 15, 25, 41, 84, 97, 112, 123, 129, 140

quantum physics, 4

resonate, 30, 38, 46, 50, 101, 104

seer, 7
self protection, 38
setting space, 33
Shaman, 34
source, 4, 10, 45, 72, 125
Spirit Box, 122
spirit communication, 21
Spirit Guides, iv, x, 27
spirits
  spirit, 7, 33, 34, 35, 73, 77, 84, 112, 113, 117, 118, 119, 121, 129, 130, 131
spiritual, iv, ix, 3, 31, 34, 41, 43, 46, 54, 73, 115, 140
spirituality, ix
Spirituality, 66

Tarot, 45, 50, 51, 53

Universal Laws, 27, 28, 30, 109
Universe, x, 27, 66, 67, 68, 83, 91, 120

Visualize, 32, 54, 99, 106

www.ingramcontent.com/pod-product-compliance
Lightning Source LLC
Chambersburg PA
CBHW052054070526
44584CB00017B/2168